barefoot contessa
at home

barefoot
contessa
at home

everyday recipes
you'll make over and over again

ina garten

Photographs by Quentin Bacon

BANTAM PRESS

LONDON · NEW YORK · TORONTO · SYDNEY · AUCKLAND

TRANSWORLD PUBLISHERS
61–63 Uxbridge Road, London W5 5SA
A Random House Group Company
www.rbooks.co.uk

First published in the United States
in 2006 by Clarkson Potter/Publishers
an imprint of the Crown Publishing Group
a division of Random House, Inc., New York

First published in Great Britain
in 2011 by Bantam Press
an imprint of Transworld Publishers

ISBN 9780593068403

Addresses for Random House Group Ltd companies outside the UK can be found at: www.randomhouse.co.uk
The Random House Group Ltd Reg. No. 954009

The Random House Group Ltd supports the Forest Stewardship Council (FSC), the leading international
forest-certification organization. All our titles that are printed on Greenpeace-approved FSC-certified paper
carry the FSC logo.
Our paper procurement policy can be found at
www.rbooks.co.uk/environment

Printed in China

2 4 6 8 10 9 7 5 3 1

CONVERSION CHART

Oven Temperatures:	Spoon Measures:	American Solid Measures:	Liquid Measures:
130°C = 250°F = Gas mark ½	1 level tablespoon flour = 15g	1 cup rice US = 225g	1 cup US = 275ml
150°C = 300°F = Gas mark 2	1 heaped tablespoon flour = 28g	1 cup flour US = 115g	1 pint US = 550ml
180°C = 350°F = Gas mark 4	1 level tablespoon sugar = 28g	1 cup butter US = 225g	1 quart US = 900ml
190°C = 375°F = Gas mark 5	1 level tablespoon butter = 15g	1 stick butter US = 115g	
200°C = 400°F = Gas mark 6		1 cup dried fruit US = 225g	
220°C = 425°F = Gas mark 7		1 cup brown sugar US = 180g	
230°C = 450°F = Gas mark 8		1 cup granulated sugar US = 225g	

My home is wherever Jeffrey is

thanks

Recently, my assistant, Barbara Libath, said that she wanted to take some recipes home to retest over the weekend. I said to her, "Are you sure you want to work over the weekend?" And she replied, "Oh, is that what we're doing . . . working?" First and foremost, I want to thank Barbara not just for being so extraordinary but also for making every day together feel as though we're just playing.

So many people helped make these books reality. My wonderful editor, Pam Krauss at Clarkson Potter/Publishers, is there for me through the highs and lows of writing cookbooks. Whenever I'm stuck, she knows exactly the right word to say to get me going again. Marysarah Quinn, who designs my books, always knows exactly the tone I'm looking for. And Esther Newberg, my amazing agent at ICM, always takes care of business so I can keep writing books. Thank you.

Thank you, too, for the fun and creative team of people that show up at my house in East Hampton to photograph my books. Rori Trovato and Megan Schlow make such beautiful food and Miguel Flores-Vianna arranges the perfect setting for it. And then Quentin Bacon takes beautiful photographs.

And finally, thank you to all my friends who inspire my cooking: Eli Zabar of E.A.T, Eli's Bread, Taste, and Eli's Manhattan; Anna Pump at Loaves & Fishes; George Germon and Johanne Killeen, chef-owners of Al Forno Restaurant in Providence, Rhode Island, and authors of the cookbook *Cucina Simpatica*; and, most of all, the talented Sarah Leah Chase, author of *The Open House Cookbook* and *Cold Weather Cooking*.

contents

intro

"Something smells really good!" my husband, Jeffrey, exclaims every Friday night when he walks in the door. Most weeks, Jeffrey has been around the world and back and when he walks in that door, I want him to feel that he's really *home.* What he doesn't realize is that what feels very casual is, in fact, quite deliberate: the music is playing, all the lights are on, there are flowers everywhere, and chicken and onions are roasting in the oven.

I didn't always know how to make a home. It took time and lots of experimentation. Over the thirty-eight years we've been married, I've tried everything—the good, the bad, and the ugly. But I've evolved a style that seems to work for me: big sofas for a nap on Sunday afternoon; comfy reading chairs with good light and a view out the window for daydreaming; great CDs piled up by the stereo; and my favorite old videos next to the television. I like knowing that there are twenty new magazines on the coffee table, delicious French teas in the pantry, and expensive bath bubbles next to the tub. A good home should gather you up in its arms like a warm cashmere blanket, soothe your hurt feelings, and prepare you to go back out into that big bad world tomorrow all ready to fight the dragons.

I'm basically a nester. All day long, I feel as though I'm batting back the baseballs that are being hurled at me: decisions to make, places to go, cranky people to deal with . . . and when I come home, I want my house to feel serene and beautiful, like the way you feel when you get into a bed piled high with down pillows: you're safe. Jeffrey and I have moved many times in the years we've been married and though we've always had a house (or at least an apartment), I've never been comfortable until I've made it a *home.* When we were first married, Jeffrey was in the Army and we moved to the less-than-cosmopolitan town of Fayetteville, North Carolina, where we rented a little furnished garden apartment. It was probably fairly ordinary, but I thought it was wonderful. The first week, I rolled up my sleeves, cleaned it from top to bottom, made curtains for the windows, painted the bedroom, bought a rug for the living room, and stocked the kitchen. We made friends in the neighborhood, gave dinner parties, and very soon we felt right at home.

After the Army, Jeffrey and I moved to Washington, D.C., where he was in graduate school and I worked for the government. Each time we moved I wanted to do even more to make us feel at home. This time, I rented an unfurnished apartment so I could also choose the furniture. I seem to remember some very

1970s black and white furniture with splashes of purple and yellow. What was I thinking?? But at the time it felt just right. The next time we moved, we bought our first house, which gave me the chance to choose the furniture *and* decorate the house. This was starting to get really challenging. Unfortunately, I was still learning. The first thing I did in the new house was paper the bedroom with a very pretty blue and white wallpaper printed with Japanese dogwood blossoms. Only when I was finished did I realize that I'd hung the paper completely upside down. I couldn't afford to redo it, so for years I woke up every morning to upside-down dogwood branches. More important, though, this was the first house in which I got to design my own kitchen from the ground up and it was the place where I really started to cook. *Mastering the Art of French Cooking,* by Julia Child, Simone Beck, and Louisette Bertholle, was my bible and my friends were my guinea pigs. I started to have parties on a regular basis and began to realize that friends were also an important part of what made a house feel like home to us.

After many years and lots of houses, we moved to the east end of Long Island. I'll never forget New Year's Day 1985. For the previous seven years, I'd owned a specialty food store in Westhampton Beach called Barefoot Contessa. Jeffrey and I were driving into East Hampton that day to see the new space that I had rented. As we drove down Montauk Highway on that bright, chilly morning through the double allée of ancient sycamore trees whose branches reach elegantly across the highway, past the picturesque town pond with ducks and swans, around the historic Mulford Farm with its perfectly preserved buildings dating back to the seventeenth century, I remember thinking that I was really, finally, home.

Twenty years later, I look back on that day and smile. When you find a chair that's comfortable, you just know it. That's how I feel about the place I live. I can't imagine being happier anywhere else. Yes, it's a place where Hollywood stars hang out with New York investment bankers. But that's not my East Hampton. For me, it's a place with a deep history and in some ways it's not all that different from the farming community it was when it was founded in 1640. It's a place where Jim Pike, who grew up in suburban Westchester County, New York, wanting to be a farmer, came to make his home and started an extraordinary farm in Sagaponack that sells heirloom tomatoes, sweet white corn, and the most delicious raspberries. It's a place where Sal and Eileen Iacono inherited a farm from their family and, realizing that vegetable farming was too tough a life, instead started raising the best chickens that ever graced a Sunday dinner. It's a place where fishermen like the Duryea family of Montauk have hauled in seafood and lobsters for three generations. Later, it became home to business people like my dear friend Antonia Bellanca, who came to set up first a flower shop and then a worldwide fragrance business called Antonia's Flowers. And lots of people who, like my friend Barbara Libath, came here for summers as children and decided to raise their families here year-round. We all came to East Hampton and found ourselves at home.

What really makes a house or apartment feel like home? For me, it's good music, great smells from the kitchen, pretty flowers, and a quiet, relaxed atmosphere. Sure, it has to make Jeffrey and me comfortable, but equally important, it has to make my friends want to drop by. Over the years, I've learned so many things that work for me. It's often said that first impressions count when you're meeting someone new and I think it's the same for a house. How people feel when they walk in the door really sets the mood. I want to appeal to all their senses. As soon as they enter the house I want them to smell something delicious, even if it's as simple as freshly brewing coffee. They should see things that are beautiful: orange tulips, antique rugs, and a quirky coat rack on which to hang their coats. But most important of all, I want them to feel my warm embrace, which I hope will make them feel right at home.

Next is the living room, where a huge farm table is set up with drinks. At a restaurant you're served, but when you're home you help yourself, so I like my guests to be able to fix their own drinks . . . I want it to feel like raiding the refrigerator. On a hot summer day, the air-conditioning is set a little too cool so it's refreshing after the heat outside. On a cold winter night, there's wood crackling in the fireplace so it's cozy and warm inside. Furniture is important, too: it should be soft and inviting—without making you want to go to sleep. The current trend is enormous sofas with big down pillows. That's great on a Sunday afternoon for a nap but if I want to sit and talk with friends, I always feel a little like Alice in Wonderland in one of those oversized pieces. Instead, I like sofas that sit like armchairs: they're very comfortable but they make you sit up. The next thing is a cocktail table: if it's too big, you can't have an intimate conversation with someone; too delicate and you can't put your feet up. In fact, my favorite "coffee table" is not a table at all; it's a huge upholstered ottoman topped with big books and a tray for drinks. The living room shouldn't be a place we use just for company or special occasions; I want it to say, "Come sit down and make yourself at home."

The dining room is next. It's not easy to make the dining room look inviting unless it's set for a party, which probably isn't all that often. I actually like a dining room that feels more like a library: a big table surrounded by walls of books. The lighting is soft, the table in the middle is long, and the chairs are comfortable for reading or eating. When I'm not having a party, I'll pile books and flowers on the table. When I am having a party, I'll put layers and layers of cloths on the table—taffeta or linen underneath and antique damask on top—and then fill the room with votive candles. Whether it's set for a party, or just waiting for me to sit down and read a book, the dining room is always cozy.

Personal details are important. How many times have you seen a gorgeous house in a shelter magazine that looks absolutely soulless? Everything's right but it's really not. That's because everything matches perfectly and the designer didn't incorporate the client's personal style—or any of those messy real things that people acquire. I had an interesting conversation recently with a renowned antiques dealer and designer. I was buying two small Chinese creamware vases from him and I asked if I should buy a third to make a grouping. He said, "No, don't buy a third one. Find a personal object in the same color or shape—a shell you found on a trip, or an interesting object you love—and put them together." I realized that that's why his rooms feel so right; they're not just beautiful but they have soul. They give a sense that a person with a full, rich life lives there.

At the end of the day, though, my house is all about the kitchen. The kitchen is like the heartbeat of the house; it's what's going on and where we always end up. I designed the kitchen to face south so that during the day it's the brightest room in the house. It also looks onto my garden, so it has the best view in the house. I organized the space to have lots of places for people to hang out without interrupting my work-space. They can sit at the table or perch on the stools while I'm cooking. They can also cook with me on the other side of the counter and not be in my way. And since most of my dinner par-ties are held in the kitchen, I can get a whole meal ready with-out ever leaving the party. The kitchen table is a forty-eight-inch round, which is ideal for four to six people. The lighting is on a dimmer so I can turn it up for working and turn it down for din-ner. The counter is close to the kitchen table; it's black granite, which not only is great for cooking and baking but also makes a terrific buffet for a dinner party. All these details look casual but they're designed with one thing in mind: if my friends come to my house and feel like family, they'll always come back for more.

For me, though, the very best way of all to make a house into a home is to have the smells of good food coming from the kitchen. I hope in this book you'll find lots of recipes you'll want to make over and over again so that everyone who comes to visit will feel as much at home as you do.

I believe in keeping cocktails simple. These are my two favorite things to serve when guests arrive.

fresh whiskey sours

MAKES 4 COCKTAILS

¾ cup	Jack Daniel's Tennessee Whiskey
½ cup	freshly squeezed lemon juice (3 lemons)
½ cup	freshly squeezed lime juice (4 limes)
⅔ cup	sugar syrup (see note)
	Maraschino cherries

Combine the whiskey, lemon juice, lime juice, and syrup. Fill a cocktail shaker halfway with ice and fill two-thirds full with the cocktail mixture. Shake for 30 seconds and pour into glasses. Add a maraschino cherry and serve ice cold.

To make sugar syrup, put 1 cup of sugar and 1 cup of water in a small saucepan and cook over medium heat until the sugar dissolves. Chill thoroughly before using.

green herb dip

MAKES 2 CUPS

8 ounces	cream cheese at room temperature
½ cup	sour cream at room temperature
½ cup	good mayonnaise
¾ cup	chopped scallions, white and green parts (3 scallions)
¼ cup	chopped fresh flat-leaf parsley
1 tablespoon	chopped fresh dill
1 teaspoon	kosher salt
¼ teaspoon	freshly ground black pepper

Place the cream cheese, sour cream, mayonnaise, scallions, parsley, dill, salt, and pepper in the bowl of food processor fitted with the steel blade. Pulse 10 to 12 times, until just blended, but not puréed. Serve at room temperature.

soup &
sandwich

california blt's

summer borscht

caesar club sandwich

mexican chicken soup

chicken salad sandwiches

ribollita

smoked salmon & egg salad tartines

fresh pea soup

garlic croutons

roasted pepper & goat cheese sandwiches

cream of wild mushroom soup

tomato, mozzarella & pesto panini

shrimp bisque

honey white bread

making a grocery list

When I lived in Washington, D.C., I used to see cute young guys roaming around the Georgetown Safeway with a grocery cart and a cookbook, trying to shop for dinner. (For that reason, it was always considered the place to find a date for Saturday night.) I remember one Capitol Hill staff guy with a cookbook in his hand and a five-pound bag of flour in his cart asking me if it was enough flour to yield ¼ cup of flour. I don't think he was trying to pick me up . . . more likely he was just looking for someone to cook him dinner.

Shopping with a cookbook is a pretty cumbersome way to shop. However, I've gotten pointers on making a grocery list from the many professional food stylists that I've worked with over the years. Here are some of the lessons I've learned:

* Take a pad of paper and make the following headings on the page: Dairy, Shelf Goods, Meat & Fish, Produce, and Freezer.
* Go through each recipe you want to make and put the ingredients you need under the appropriate heading. If you're not sure, add a Miscellaneous column.
* When you're writing the items you need on the list, write *1 jar* or *1 onion* if you need less than 1—for example, write Dijon mustard if you only need 1 tablespoon.

If you need a lot, write *12 ounces olive oil* so you don't buy an 8-ounce bottle and find you need to run back to the store in the middle of making a recipe, which is totally annoying.

- Take your grocery list and a pen to the store so you can cross off the things you've put in the basket. This way, I find I'm not re-reading the list over and over again to be sure I haven't forgotten something.

- If you're going to be shopping in several places and won't be home for more than an hour (30 minutes in the summer), place a picnic cooler with freezer bags in the trunk of your car and keep perishables such as meat cool while making all your stops. There's no point in buying good ingredients if they're going to spoil on the way home!

These may seem like simple, obvious things, but I find they make an enormous difference in the amount of time and the frustration level involved in shopping for ingredients. The way I see it, the sooner I'm finished with the shopping, the sooner I get to do the fun stuff—cooking!

california blt's

MAKES 4 SANDWICHES

I love a good bacon, lettuce, and tomato sandwich, but this is even better. It seems like an ordinary everyday lunch except when you use really good ingredients . . . and the avocado puts it right over the top. I serve these for Sunday lunch parties and people go nuts.

12	thick-cut slices smoked bacon
8 slices	good white bread, cut ½-inch thick
½ cup	good mayonnaise, such as Hellmann's
4 to 8	tender green lettuce leaves, washed and spun very dry
2	ripe Hass avocados
	juice of 1 lemon
2 large	ripe tomatoes, thickly sliced
	kosher salt and freshly ground black pepper

For the bread, I use bakery white bread or Pepperidge Farm Hearty White.

Preheat the oven to 400 degrees. Place a baking rack on a sheet pan and arrange the bacon on the rack in a single layer. Bake for 15 to 25 minutes, until the bacon is browned and crisp. Drain on paper towels and set aside.

Place 8 slices of bread on a sheet pan and toast them for 5 minutes. Turn the slices and toast for 1 more minute, until all the bread is evenly browned. Place 4 slices on a cutting board. Spread each slice with about 1 tablespoon of mayonnaise. Cover the slices with a layer of lettuce. Place 3 slices of bacon on each sandwich. Peel the avocados and slice them ½-inch thick. Toss the avocado slices gently with the lemon juice and arrange on top of the bacon. Add a layer of tomato slices and sprinkle liberally with salt and pepper.

Spread each of the remaining 4 pieces of toasted bread with 1 tablespoon of mayonnaise and place, mayonnaise side down, on the sandwiches.

summer borscht

SERVES 6

Borscht is an old-fashioned peasant soup that originated in Russia, where my grandmother was born. There are two kinds: when it's made with chunks of beef and beef stock and served hot, it can be a hearty winter soup. This lighter version, however, is made with fresh beets and chicken stock and it's served cold with a dollop of sour cream. This recipe was inspired by soup I've always loved at Loaves & Fishes.

5 medium	fresh beets (about 2 pounds without tops)
	kosher salt
2 cups	chicken stock, preferably homemade (page 45)
16 ounces	sour cream, plus extra for serving
½ cup	plain yogurt
¼ cup	sugar
2 tablespoons	freshly squeezed lemon juice
2 teaspoons	champagne vinegar
1½ teaspoons	freshly ground black pepper
2 cups	medium-diced English cucumber, seeds removed
½ cup	chopped scallions, white and green parts
2 tablespoons	chopped fresh dill, plus extra for serving

To dice the cucumbers, halve the unpeeled cucumbers lengthwise and scoop out the seeds with a teaspoon. Cut each in half again lengthwise and then dice.

When I don't have time to make homemade chicken stock, I use College Inn chicken broth instead.

Place the beets in a large pot of boiling salted water and cook uncovered until the beets are tender, 30 to 40 minutes. Remove the beets to a bowl with a slotted spoon and set aside to cool. Strain the cooking liquid through a fine sieve and also set aside to cool.

In a large bowl, whisk together 1½ cups of the beet cooking liquid, the chicken stock, sour cream, yogurt, sugar, lemon juice, vinegar, 1 tablespoon salt, and the pepper. Peel the cooled beets with a small paring knife or rub the skins off with your hands. Cut the beets in a small to medium dice. Add the beets, cucumber, scallions, and dill to the soup. Cover with plastic wrap and chill for at least 4 hours or overnight. Season to taste and serve cold with a dollop of sour cream and an extra sprig of fresh dill.

caesar club sandwich

SERVES 3

Here's another example of how I like to deconstruct a familiar dish and reassemble it into something new. I make a Caesar salad with pancetta and croutons, so I thought, "Why not make a Caesar sandwich with the 'croutons' on the outside?" That ultimately evolved into a Caesar Club Sandwich with chicken. The ciabatta I use is a 4 × 10-inch rectangle. If your bread is a different size, adjust the recipe accordingly.

2 split (1 whole)	chicken breasts, bone in, skin on
	good olive oil
	kosher salt and freshly ground black pepper
4 ounces	thinly sliced pancetta
1 large	garlic clove, chopped
2 tablespoons	chopped fresh flat-leaf parsley
1½ teaspoons	anchovy paste
1 teaspoon	Dijon mustard
1½ tablespoons	freshly squeezed lemon juice
½ cup	good mayonnaise
1 large	ciabatta bread
2 ounces	baby arugula, washed and spun dry
12	sun-dried tomatoes in oil
2 to 3 ounces	Parmesan, shaved

Preheat the oven to 350 degrees.

Place the chicken breasts on a sheet pan skin side up. Rub the chicken with olive oil and sprinkle with salt and pepper. Roast for 35 to 40 minutes, until cooked through. Cool slightly, discard the skin and bones, and slice the meat thickly. Set aside.

Meanwhile, place the pancetta on another sheet pan in a single layer. Roast for 10 to 15 minutes, until crisp. Set aside to drain on paper towels.

Place the garlic and parsley in the bowl of a food processor fitted with a steel blade and process until minced. Add the anchovy paste, mustard, lemon juice, and mayonnaise and process again to make a smooth dressing. (Refrigerate the Caesar dressing if not using it immediately.)

Slice the ciabatta in half horizontally and separate the top from the bottom. Toast the bread in the oven, cut side up, for 5 to 7 minutes; cool slightly. Spread the cut sides of each piece with the Caesar dressing. Place half the arugula on the bottom piece of bread and then layer in order: the sun-dried tomatoes, shaved Parmesan, crispy pancetta, and sliced chicken. Sprinkle with salt and pepper and finish with another layer of arugula. Place the top slice of ciabatta on top and cut in thirds crosswise. Serve at room temperature.

mexican chicken soup

SERVES 6 TO 8

As much as I love Mexican food, I always hesitate to order it in restaurants because of my aversion to cilantro. So many people have raved about Mexican chicken soup, though, that I decided to try making it at home. It's really delicious—and, of course, you can always add cilantro. (For photograph, see page 24.)

(For photograph, see page 24.)

To crush whole tomatoes, you can either crush them with your hand or pulse them a few times in the bowl of a food processor fitted with a steel blade.

Be very careful handling jalapeños! Cut them in half, scrape out the seeds, and cut them into a small dice. Wash your hands after working with the peppers.

If you want to make your own tortilla chips for garnish, cut 3 corn tortillas in strips and fry in olive oil over medium heat until golden brown. Drain on paper towels.

4 split (2 whole)	chicken breasts, bone in, skin on
	good olive oil
	kosher salt and freshly ground black pepper
2 cups	chopped yellow onions (2 onions)
1 cup	chopped celery (2 stalks)
2 cups	chopped carrots (4 carrots)
4	large garlic cloves, chopped
2½ quarts	chicken stock, preferably homemade (page 45)
1 (28-ounce) can	whole tomatoes in purée, crushed
2 to 4	jalapeño peppers, seeded and minced
1 teaspoon	ground cumin
1 teaspoon	ground coriander seed
¼ to ½ cup	chopped fresh cilantro (optional)
6 (6-inch)	fresh white corn tortillas

To serve

sliced avocado

sour cream

grated Cheddar cheese

tortilla chips

Preheat the oven to 350 degrees. Place the chicken breasts skin side up on a sheet pan. Rub with olive oil, sprinkle with salt and pepper, and roast for 35 to 40 minutes, until done. When the chicken is cool enough to handle, discard the skin and bones, and shred the meat. Cover and set aside.

Meanwhile, heat 3 tablespoons of olive oil in a large pot or Dutch oven. Add the onions, celery, and carrots and cook over medium-low heat for 10 minutes, or until the onions start to brown. Add the garlic and cook for 30 seconds. Add the chicken stock, tomatoes with their purée, jalapeños, cumin, coriander, 1 tablespoon salt (depending on the saltiness of the chicken stock), 1 teaspoon pepper, and the cilantro, if using. Cut the tortillas in half, then cut them crosswise into ½-inch strips and add to the soup. Bring the soup to a boil, then lower the heat and simmer for 25 minutes. Add the shredded chicken and season to taste. Serve the soup hot topped with sliced avocado, a dollop of sour cream, grated Cheddar cheese, and broken tortilla chips.

chicken salad sandwiches

SERVES 4 TO 5

No one makes sandwiches like Eli Zabar; they're the classics but with the volume turned up. This sandwich is inspired by his tarragon chicken salad. I roast the chicken rather than poaching it to ensure that the meat stays moist and delicious.

4 split (2 whole)	chicken breasts, bone in, skin on
	good olive oil
	kosher salt and freshly ground black pepper
¾ cup	good mayonnaise, plus more for the bread
1½ tablespoons	chopped fresh tarragon leaves
1 cup	small-diced celery (2 stalks)
8 to 10 slices	health or seven-grain bread
1 package	mesclun salad mix

Preheat the oven to 350 degrees.

Place the chicken breasts, skin side up, on a sheet pan and rub them with olive oil. Sprinkle generously with salt and pepper. Roast for 35 to 40 minutes, until the chicken is cooked through. Set aside to cool.

When the chicken is cool, remove and discard the skin and bones and cut the chicken into ¾-inch dice. Place the chicken in a bowl and add the mayonnaise, tarragon, celery, 2 teaspoons salt, and 1 teaspoon pepper and toss well.

To assemble, spread a little mayonnaise on half the bread slices, top with the chicken salad and mesclun mix, and cover with the remaining slices of bread. Cut in half and serve.

ribollita

SERVES 6 TO 8

Ribollita *literally means "twice boiled" in Italian and it's the old-fashioned way to use up all the leftover vegetables and bread from the week. Every ribollita has its own character; I've added some pancetta and good chicken stock to give mine lots of flavor. With a sprinkling of Parmesan cheese and a drizzle of olive oil, it's the perfect hearty Sunday night dinner.*

½ pound	dried white beans, such as Great Northern or cannellini
	kosher salt
¼ cup	good olive oil, plus extra for serving
¼ pound	large-diced pancetta or smoked bacon
2 cups	chopped yellow onions (2 onions)
1 cup	chopped carrots (3 carrots)
1 cup	chopped celery (3 stalks)
3 tablespoons	minced garlic (6 cloves)
1 teaspoon	freshly ground black pepper
¼ teaspoon	crushed red pepper flakes
1 (28-ounce) can	Italian plum tomatoes in purée, chopped
4 cups	coarsely chopped or shredded Savoy cabbage (optional)
4 cups	coarsely chopped kale
½ cup	chopped fresh basil leaves
6 cups	chicken stock, preferably homemade (page 45)
4 cups	sourdough bread cubes, crusts removed
½ cup	freshly grated Parmesan cheese, for serving

In a large bowl, cover the beans with cold water by 1 inch and cover with plastic wrap. Allow to soak overnight in the refrigerator.

Drain the beans, place them in a large pot with 8 cups water, and bring to a boil. Lower the heat and simmer uncovered for 45 minutes. Add 1 teaspoon of salt and continue to simmer for about 15 minutes, until the beans are tender. Set the beans aside to cool in their liquid.

Meanwhile, heat the oil in a large stockpot. Add the pancetta and onions and cook over medium-low heat for 7 to 10 minutes, until the onions are translucent. Add the carrots, celery, garlic, 1 tablespoon of salt, the pepper, and red pepper flakes. Cook over medium-low heat for 7 to 10 minutes, until the vegetables are tender. Add the tomatoes with their purée, the cabbage, if using, the kale, and basil and cook over medium-low heat, stirring occasionally, for another 7 to 10 minutes.

Drain the beans, reserving their cooking liquid. In the bowl of a food processor fitted with a steel blade, purée half of the beans with a little of their liquid. Add to the stockpot, along with the remaining whole beans. Pour the bean cooking liquid into a large measuring cup and add enough chicken stock to make 8 cups. Add to the soup and bring to a boil. Reduce the heat and simmer over low heat for 20 minutes.

Add the bread to the soup and simmer for 10 more minutes. Taste for seasoning and serve hot in large bowls sprinkled with Parmesan cheese and drizzled with olive oil.

This soup is even better the next day but it gets very thick. Add some water or chicken stock, if needed.

If you can find kale, it adds flavor and texture to the soup.

smoked salmon & egg salad tartines

SERVES 8

Everyone has a secret "feel-good" food, and mine is egg salad. Anyone can make a perfectly fine egg salad, but I like mine with mustard and lots of fresh dill. When I'm tired and cranky, a simple egg salad sandwich on white bread is the perfect lunch to change my mood. For company, I take it to the next level with smoked salmon and whole-grain bread.

I use extra-large eggs because they're a better value per pound. You can certainly use large eggs instead.

Smoked salmon is sometimes referred to as "lox," but lox is really salt-cured rather than smoked. Look for Norwegian or Scottish salmon, if you can find it.

12	extra-large eggs
⅓ cup	good mayonnaise
2 teaspoons	whole-grain mustard
1 tablespoon	minced fresh dill, plus sprigs for garnish
1 teaspoon	kosher salt
½ teaspoon	freshly ground black pepper
8 slices	7-grain bread or round French bread (*boule*)
8 slices	good smoked salmon

Place the eggs in a large pot and cover them with cool tap water. Bring the water to a boil, lower the heat, and simmer for 5 minutes. Turn off the heat and allow the eggs to sit in the water for another 5 minutes. Drain, then fill the pot with cold water. To peel the eggs, tap each end on a board, then roll the egg between your hand and the board to crackle the shell. Peel under running tap water and allow the eggs to cool to room temperature.

Place the eggs in the bowl of a food processor fitted with a steel blade. Pulse the processor 10 to 12 times to break up, but not purée, the eggs. Transfer the chopped eggs to a bowl and add the mayonnaise, mustard, dill, salt, and pepper. Combine lightly with a fork.

Toast or grill the bread. Lay one slice of salmon on each piece of bread, spread on the egg salad, then garnish with a sprig of dill. Serve at room temperature.

fresh pea soup

SERVES 6

This is a soup that can be served hot or cold. If you plan to chill it, make it early and let the flavors meld in the refrigerator. Hot or cold, I think the mint really wakes up the flavor of the peas. If you can't find fresh peas, frozen peas are just fine!

2 tablespoons	unsalted butter
2 cups	chopped leeks, white and light green parts (2 leeks)
1 cup	chopped yellow onion
4 cups	chicken stock, preferably homemade (page 45)
5 cups	freshly shelled peas or 2 (10-ounce) packages frozen peas
⅔ cup	chopped fresh mint leaves, loosely packed
2 teaspoons	kosher salt
½ teaspoon	freshly ground black pepper
½ cup	crème fraîche
½ cup	chopped fresh chives
	Garlic Croutons, for serving (page 44)

To clean leeks, chop well and then soak in a bowl of water for a few minutes. Lift the leeks from the bowl to be sure any sand is left behind.

Four pounds of peas in the pod will yield about 5 cups of shelled peas.

Heat the butter in a large saucepan, add the leeks and onion, and cook over medium-low heat for 5 to 10 minutes, until the onion is tender. Add the chicken stock, increase the heat to high, and bring to a boil. Add the peas and cook for 3 to 5 minutes, until the peas are tender. (Frozen peas will take only 3 minutes.) Off the heat, add the mint, salt, and pepper.

Purée the soup in batches: place 1 cup of soup in a blender, place the lid on top, and purée on low speed. With the blender still running, open the venthole in the lid and slowly add more soup until the blender is three-quarters full. Pour the soup into a large bowl and repeat until all the soup is puréed. Whisk in the crème fraîche and chives and taste for seasoning. Serve hot with garlic croutons.

garlic croutons

MAKES 2 CUPS

I always have some kind of leftover bread in the freezer and this is a good way to use it up. If you have a rustic Italian or French bread, it will make earthy, crunchy croutons, but sometimes I like a more refined crouton. In that case, I choose a finer-crumbed bakery white bread. I especially like the crunch of a crouton on a creamy soup like hot shrimp bisque or a chilled fresh pea soup.

For homemade white bread, see the recipe on page 57

½ loaf	good bakery white bread, sliced ½-inch thick
1 large	garlic clove
2 tablespoons	good olive oil
	kosher salt and freshly ground black pepper

Remove the crusts from the bread slices and cut into ½-inch cubes.

Crush the garlic with the side of a large chef's knife and discard the peel. In a medium sauté pan, heat the oil over medium heat and add the garlic. Cook for about 1 minute, until the garlic starts to brown, and then discard the garlic. Add the bread cubes, sprinkle with salt and pepper, and cook over medium heat, tossing occasionally, until browned on all sides.

chicken stock

MAKES 6 QUARTS

3 (5-pound)	whole roasting chickens
3 large	yellow onions, unpeeled, quartered
6	carrots, unpeeled, halved
4	celery stalks with leaves, cut into thirds
4	parsnips, unpeeled, cut in half (optional)
20 sprigs	fresh flat-leaf parsley
15 sprigs	fresh thyme
20 sprigs	fresh dill
1 head	garlic, unpeeled, cut in half crosswise
2 tablespoons	kosher salt
2 teaspoons	whole black peppercorns

Place the chickens, onions, carrots, celery, parsnips, if using, parsley, thyme, dill, garlic, salt, and pepper in a 16- to 20-quart stockpot. Add 7 quarts water and bring to a boil. Simmer uncovered for 4 hours. Strain the entire contents of the pot through a colander and discard the solids. Pack in quart containers and chill overnight. Refrigerate for up to 5 days or freeze for up to 6 months.

roasted pepper & goat cheese sandwiches

SERVES 4 TO 6

I always thought roasting peppers over an open gas flame and then peeling them was an annoying job until my television producer, Olivia Grove, showed me how to roast them in the oven—it's so much easier. Now I keep a container of roasted peppers in the refrigerator ready to make this delicious sandwich any time.

4 large	red or yellow bell peppers, preferably Holland
2 tablespoons	good olive oil
1 tablespoon	balsamic vinegar
2	garlic cloves, minced
2 teaspoons	kosher salt
1 teaspoon	freshly ground black pepper
2 tablespoons	drained capers

For assembling

1 large	ciabatta bread, halved horizontally
1 (11-ounce)	garlic-and-herb Montrachet or plain goat cheese, at room temperature
8 to 10 large	basil leaves
3 thin slices	red onion
	kosher salt and freshly ground black pepper

Capers are the flower bud of a bush mostly found in the Mediterranean. The buds are usually pickled in brine, but sometimes they're packed in salt. Wash the salted ones before using.

Balsamic vinegar is made from white wine vinegar that gets its dark color, intense flavor, and syrupy consistency from being aged in wood barrels for years. As with wine, the longer it's aged, the more deeply flavored the vinegar.

Preheat the oven to 500 degrees.

Place the whole peppers on a sheet pan and place in the oven for 30 to 40 minutes, until the skins are completely wrinkled and the peppers are charred, turning them twice during roasting. Remove the pan from the oven and immediately cover it tightly with aluminum foil. Set aside for 30 minutes, or until the peppers are cool enough to handle.

Meanwhile, combine the olive oil, balsamic vinegar, garlic, salt, and pepper in a small bowl. Set aside.

Remove the stem from each pepper and cut them in quarters. Remove the peels and seeds and place the peppers in a bowl along with any juices that have collected. Discard the stems, peels, and seeds. Pour the oil and vinegar mixture over the peppers. Stir in the capers. Cover with plastic wrap and refrigerate for a few hours to allow the flavors to blend.

To assemble the sandwiches, spread the bottom half of the loaf with the goat cheese. Add a layer of peppers and then a layer of basil leaves. Separate the onions into rings and spread out on top. Sprinkle with salt and pepper. Top with the top half of the ciabatta and cut into individual servings.

cream of wild mushroom soup

SERVES 5 TO 6

Parker Hodges was the chef at Barefoot Contessa and he made this delicious soup all winter long. It was especially popular for the holidays when wild mushrooms are in season. Though technically these mushrooms are cultivated, not "wild," they have much more flavor than regular button mushrooms. Don't substitute dried mushrooms because the flavor and texture of fresh mushrooms are important to this soup. If you can't find exactly this mixture, use 15 ounces of any "wild" mushrooms that are available.

5 ounces	fresh shiitake mushrooms
5 ounces	fresh portobello mushrooms
5 ounces	fresh cremini (or porcini) mushrooms
1 tablespoon	good olive oil
¼ pound (1 stick) plus 1 tablespoon	unsalted butter
1 cup	chopped yellow onion
1	carrot, chopped
1	sprig of fresh thyme plus 1 teaspoon minced thyme leaves
	kosher salt and freshly ground black pepper
2 cups	chopped leeks, white and light green parts (2 leeks)
¼ cup	all-purpose flour
1 cup	dry white wine
1 cup	half-and-half
1 cup	heavy cream
½ cup	minced fresh flat-leaf parsley

Clean the mushrooms by wiping them with a dry paper towel. Don't wash them! Separate the stems, trim off any bad parts, and coarsely chop the stems. Slice the mushroom caps ¼-inch thick and, if they are big, cut them into bite-size pieces. Set aside.

To make the stock, heat the olive oil and 1 tablespoon of the butter in a large pot. Add the chopped mushroom stems, the onion, carrot, the sprig of thyme, 1 teaspoon salt, and ½ teaspoon pepper and cook over medium-low heat for 10 to 15 minutes, until the vegetables are soft. Add 6 cups water, bring to a boil, reduce the heat, and simmer uncovered for 30 minutes. Strain, reserving the liquid. You should have about 4½ cups of stock. If not, add some water.

Meanwhile, in another large pot, heat the remaining ¼ pound of butter and add the leeks. Cook over low heat for 15 to 20 minutes, until the leeks begin to brown. Add the sliced mushroom caps and cook for 10 minutes, or until they are browned and tender. Add the flour and cook for 1 minute. Add the white wine and stir for another minute, scraping the bottom of the pot. Add the mushroom stock, minced thyme leaves, 1½ teaspoons salt, and 1 teaspoon pepper and bring to a boil. Reduce the heat and simmer for 15 minutes. Add the half-and-half, cream, and parsley, season to taste, and heat through but do not boil. Serve hot.

tomato, mozzarella & pesto panini

MAKES 6 SANDWICHES

I'm not big on specialized equipment; why have three things that smash garlic when the back of the knife I already own does the same thing? But one day I decided I just had to buy a panini machine and boy, am I glad I did! It's a great way to make delicious hot sandwiches for lunch. You can also make dessert sandwiches with slices of brioche bread and good chocolate melted in the middle. Yum.

2 large	ripe beefsteak tomatoes
1 (16-ounce) ball	fresh mozzarella
12 slices	bakery white bread, sliced ½-inch thick
about 1 cup	prepared pesto
	kosher salt
	unsalted butter, at room temperature

Preheat a panini grill machine.

Core the tomatoes and slice the tomatoes and mozzarella ¼-inch thick.

Place the bread slices on a work surface. Spread each slice evenly with pesto. Place a layer of mozzarella (about 2 slices) on half of the bread and cover with a layer of tomato. (If the tomatoes are large, it will only be one slice.) Sprinkle the tomato with salt. Place the remaining slices of bread, pesto side down, on top. Spread the top and bottom of each sandwich with softened butter. Grill the sandwiches in batches on the panini grill for 2 to 3 minutes, until the mozzarella starts to ooze. Cut each sandwich in half, and serve warm.

You can assemble the sandwiches in advance and grill them before serving.

If you don't have a panini grill, you can use a stovetop grill and weight the sandwiches with a plate.

shrimp bisque

SERVES 4 TO 6

I had always avoided making bisques because they invariably require a million steps. Since I came up with this easier—but still rich and delicious—version, I find that I make it over and over again.

1 pound	large shrimp, peeled and deveined, shells reserved
4 cups	seafood stock (page 55)
3 tablespoons	good olive oil
2 cups	chopped leeks, white and light green parts (3 leeks)
1 tablespoon	chopped garlic (3 cloves)
	pinch of cayenne pepper
¼ cup	Cognac or brandy
¼ cup	dry sherry
4 tablespoons (½ stick)	unsalted butter
¼ cup	all-purpose flour
2 cups	half-and-half
⅓ cup	tomato paste
2 teaspoons	kosher salt
1 teaspoon	freshly ground black pepper

Place the shrimp shells and seafood stock in a saucepan and simmer for 15 minutes. Strain and reserve the stock. Add enough water to make 3¾ cups.

Meanwhile, heat the olive oil in a large pot or Dutch oven. Add the leeks and cook them for 10 minutes over medium-low heat, or until the leeks are tender but not browned. Add the garlic and cook for 1 more minute. Add the cayenne pepper and shrimp and cook over medium to low heat for 3 minutes, stirring occasionally. Add the Cognac and cook for 1 minute, then the

sherry and cook for 3 minutes longer. Transfer the shrimp and leeks to a food processor fitted with a steel blade and process until coarsely puréed.

In the same pot, melt the butter. Add the flour and cook over medium-low heat for 1 minute, stirring with a wooden spoon. Add the half-and-half and cook, stirring with a whisk, until thickened, about 3 minutes. Stir in the puréed shrimp, the stock, tomato paste, salt, and pepper and heat gently until hot but not boiling. Season to taste and serve hot.

seafood stock

MAKES ABOUT 1 QUART

You can make this stock in advance; it freezes beautifully.

2 tablespoons	good olive oil
1½ cups	shrimp shells (from about a pound of shrimp)
2 cups	chopped yellow onions (2 onions)
2	carrots, unpeeled and chopped
3 stalks	celery, chopped
2 cloves	garlic, minced
½ cup	good white wine
⅓ cup	tomato paste
1 tablespoon	kosher salt
1½ teaspoons	freshly ground black pepper
10 sprigs	fresh thyme, including stems

Warm the oil in a stockpot over medium heat. Add the shrimp shells, onions, carrots, and celery and sauté for 15 minutes, until lightly browned. Add the garlic and cook for 2 more minutes. Add 1½ quarts of water, the white wine, tomato paste, salt, pepper, and thyme. Bring to a boil, then reduce the heat and simmer for 1 hour. Strain through a sieve, pressing the solids. You should have approximately 1 quart of stock. You can make up the difference with water or wine if needed.

honey white bread

MAKES 2 LOAVES

*So many of my dishes call for "good white bread" and many people
have e-mailed me to say they have trouble finding it. I don't usually
spend time making bread, but this recipe is foolproof. Baking two loaves
means you'll have one for now and one for the freezer.*

½ cup	warm water (110 degrees)
2 packages	dry yeast
1 teaspoon	sugar
1½ cups	warm whole milk (110 degrees)
6 tablespoons (¾ stick)	unsalted butter, melted and cooled
1½ tablespoons	honey
2	extra-large egg yolks
5 to 6 cups	all-purpose flour
1 tablespoon	kosher salt
1	egg white, lightly beaten

Place the water in the bowl of an electric mixer fitted with a
dough hook attachment. If the bowl is cold, be sure the water
temperature doesn't drop below 110 degrees. Add the yeast and
sugar; stir and allow them to dissolve for 5 minutes.

Add the milk, butter, and honey. Mix on medium speed until
blended. Add the egg yolks, 3 cups of the flour, and the salt. Mix
on low speed for about 5 minutes. With the mixer still on low
speed, add 2 more cups of flour. Raise the speed to medium and
slowly add just enough of the remaining flour so the dough
doesn't stick to the bowl. Add the flour slowly; you can always
add more but you can't take it out. Knead on medium speed for
about 8 minutes, adding flour as necessary.

Dump the dough out onto a floured surface and knead by hand for a minute, until the dough is smooth and elastic. Grease a bowl with butter, put the dough in the bowl, then turn it over so the top is lightly buttered. Cover the bowl with a damp towel and allow it to rise for 1 hour, until doubled in volume.

Grease two 9 × 5-inch loaf pans with butter. Divide the dough in half, roll each half into a loaf shape and place each in a prepared pan. Cover again with the damp towel, and allow to rise again for an hour, until doubled in volume.

Meanwhile, preheat the oven to 350 degrees. When the dough is ready, brush the tops with the egg white and bake the breads for 40 to 45 minutes, until they sound hollow when tapped. Turn them out of the pans and cool completely on a wire rack before slicing.

salads

heirloom tomatoes with blue cheese dressing

chicken salad véronique

grilled tuna salad

bibb salad with basil green goddess dressing

jon snow's fish salad

roasted shrimp & orzo

pesto pea salad

warm duck salad

tomato feta salad

blue cheese coleslaw

guacamole salad

old-fashioned potato salad

outdoor parties

Years ago, when I was a caterer, a bride told me that she wanted to have her May wedding outdoors by the pool. It sounds like a beautiful, romantic idea but the reality of it is just so risky. I tactfully explained to her that if the temperature was above seventy-five degrees, they'd swelter with no shade from the sun; below sixty-eight degrees and the wedding guests would freeze. That's a pretty small window of comfort—never mind the possibility of a downpour or high winds! Unfortunately she wouldn't be dissuaded and as I had anticipated, when the sun went down, the evening chill set in. I'll never forget the image of elegant guests in tuxedos and long gowns picking up their dinner tables (set for ten with wine glasses and dinner plates!) and tilting them through the front door of her house. Not a good idea.

Outdoor parties can be really wonderful when they click. The sun is soft, the flowers are fragrant, and the gentle breeze in your hair feels so good. The key is to have a contingency plan.

Plan an outdoor party as though it's going to be a perfectly gorgeous night. Then, start all over again and plan the entire party as though you're expecting a hurricane. If you can easily imagine both scenarios, you're ready for your outdoor party.

If the party is to be held during the day and it's for more than just a few guests,

rent a tent. If it's a beautiful day, you can take the sides off the tent and make it a floating white canopy, but if the weather is bad, the sides will protect everyone. I think the structure of a tent actually makes the party cozier, making everyone feel they're at one event rather than scattered randomly around the garden.

Second, I plan a menu that I know will work outside. At one outdoor party we served a lovely cold soup and the breeze lifted the corners of the tablecloth into each soup bowl before people sat down. We didn't do that again! I tend to serve grilled fish with fresh salads and vegetables. An outdoor buffet tends to attract uninvited critters, so it's best to serve food that's already plated. Finally, featuring room-temperature food such as grilled tuna salad or summer tomato pasta helps so the meal doesn't have to be kept hot or cold while the plates are transported from the kitchen.

My friend Patricia Wells recently hosted a Sunday lunch at her farmhouse in Provence. The weather was heavenly, the guests were interesting, and lunch was served on a long table under an ancient oak tree. The meal, of course, was sublime. All afternoon the guests kept elbowing each other, saying "Isn't this amazing?" And it was. When all the elements are right, an outdoor party can really be memorable, and as long as you have a backup plan, you're safe. Remember, it's not about the setting, it's about the friends.

heirloom tomatoes with blue cheese dressing

SERVES 6 TO 8

When tomatoes are ripe in the summer, this is the simplest and most delicious salad to make. It has only a few ingredients, so choose ripe tomatoes and good French Roquefort. For interest and flavor, I like to mix thick slices of red and yellow tomatoes, wedges of green zebras (if you can find them), and halved cherry tomatoes.

3 pounds	heirloom tomatoes, mixed colors and sizes
	kosher salt and freshly ground black pepper
½ pound	Roquefort cheese, divided
1 cup	good mayonnaise
⅓ cup	heavy cream
2 teaspoons	tarragon wine vinegar
2 tablespoons	chopped fresh flat-leaf parsley (optional)

Don't refrigerate tomatoes; store them at room temperature.

If you can't find Roquefort, use another good crumbly blue cheese, such as Danish blue.

Core the tomatoes and cut the large ones into thick slices; halve or quarter the small ones. Arrange artfully on a platter and sprinkle liberally with salt and pepper.

For the dressing, place half the Roquefort cheese, the mayonnaise, heavy cream, vinegar, 1 teaspoon salt, and ½ teaspoon pepper in the bowl of a food processor fitted with a steel blade and process until combined but still chunky.

Drizzle the dressing over the tomatoes. Crumble the remaining blue cheese over the tomatoes. Sprinkle with the parsley, if using, and serve at room temperature.

chicken salad véronique

SERVES 4

This is a refreshing summer salad that we made for years at Barefoot Contessa. The combination of green tarragon, green celery, and green grapes not only looks great but the flavors are also wonderful together. If you like crunch, add toasted pecans.

4 split (2 whole)	chicken breasts, bone in, skin on
	good olive oil
	kosher salt and freshly ground black pepper
½ cup	good mayonnaise
1½ tablespoons	chopped fresh tarragon leaves
1 cup	small-diced celery (2 stalks)
1 cup	green grapes, cut in half

I prefer Hellmann's, Best, or Duke's mayonnaise.

Preheat the oven to 350 degrees.

Place the chicken breasts, skin side up, on a sheet pan and rub them with olive oil. Sprinkle generously with salt and pepper. Roast for 35 to 40 minutes, until the chicken is cooked through. Set aside until cool.

When the chicken is cool, remove the meat from the bones and discard the skin and bones. Cut the chicken into a ¾-inch dice. Place the chicken in a bowl; add the mayonnaise, tarragon leaves, celery, grapes, 1½ to 2 teaspoons salt, and 1 teaspoon pepper and toss well.

grilled tuna salad

SERVES 4 TO 5

There's nothing really wrong with tuna salad made from canned tuna, mayonnaise, and celery, but I thought something so familiar might even be better made with fresh ingredients. This is thick bites of seared fresh tuna tossed with lime juice, avocados, red onion, and scallions. After trying this, you may never go back to canned tuna.

Buy avocados in advance and allow them to ripen at room temperature. Once they're ripe, you can refrigerate them for a few days.

To prepare the avocados, cut them in half and remove the seed, then carefully ease the flesh out of the rind. Place the halves on a cutting board and dice them. Coat them immediately with extra lime juice or the vinaigrette to keep them from turning brown.

2 pounds	very fresh tuna steak, 1-inch thick
	good olive oil
	kosher salt and freshly ground black pepper
	grated zest of 2 limes
6 tablespoons	freshly squeezed lime juice (3 limes)
1 teaspoon	wasabi powder
2 teaspoons	soy sauce
10 dashes	Tabasco sauce
2	firm, ripe Hass avocados, large-diced
½	red onion, thinly sliced
¼ cup	minced scallions, white and green parts (2 scallions)
1 to 2 tablespoons	toasted sesame seeds

Heat a charcoal grill with hot coals. Brush the grill with oil.

Brush both sides of the tuna with olive oil and sprinkle generously with salt and pepper. Cook the tuna over the hot coals for about 2½ minutes on each side. Remove to a plate. The tuna should be seared on the outside and raw inside. Allow to cool slightly and cut into large bite-size cubes.

(If you don't want to heat a grill, you can sear the tuna in a dry sauté pan over high heat. Heat the pan for 2 minutes, add the tuna steaks, and cook for 2 to 3 minutes on each side, until seared on the outside and still raw inside.)

For the dressing, in a small bowl, whisk together ¼ cup of olive oil, the lime zest, lime juice, wasabi powder, soy sauce,

Tabasco, 2½ teaspoons kosher salt, and ½ teaspoon pepper. Toss the avocados in the dressing and then arrange the avocados, tuna, and red onion on individual plates. Drizzle with more dressing and sprinkle with scallions and toasted sesame seeds. Serve at room temperature.

To toast sesame seeds, place them in a dry sauté pan and cook over low heat for 5 to 10 minutes, tossing often, until the seeds turn a golden brown. Remove from the pan immediately.

bibb salad with basil green goddess dressing

SERVES 6

Green goddess dressing was invented in the 1920s at San Francisco's Palace Hotel as a tribute to William Archer's hit play, The Green Goddess. *It gets its bright green color from lots of fresh green herbs. The dressing was originally made with tarragon, but I've updated it with basil, which has more flavor. It's delicious on a green salad, but I also serve it with vegetables like blanched asparagus and broccoli.*

1 cup	good mayonnaise
1 cup	chopped scallions, white and green parts (6 to 7 scallions)
1 cup	chopped fresh basil leaves
¼ cup	freshly squeezed lemon juice (2 lemons)
2 teaspoons	chopped garlic (2 cloves)
2 teaspoons	anchovy paste
2 teaspoons	kosher salt
1 teaspoon	freshly ground black pepper
1 cup	sour cream
3 heads	Bibb lettuce
2 to 3	tomatoes

Place the mayonnaise, scallions, basil, lemon juice, garlic, anchovy paste, salt, and pepper in a blender and blend until smooth. Add the sour cream and process just until blended. (If not using immediately, refrigerate the dressing until ready to serve.)

Cut each head of lettuce into quarters, remove some of the cores, and arrange on 6 salad plates. Cut the tomatoes into wedges and add to the plates. Pour on the dressing and serve.

jon snow's
fish salad

SERVES 4 TO 5

I love when recipes are handed down from generation to generation because it means they really work. This salad is based on one made by Jon Snow, who owned a fish store in Sagaponack called Loaves & Fishes. My friend Devon Fredericks bought that shop in the mid-1970s and turned it into a specialty food store, and then she sold it to my friend Anna Pump. But they all kept making Jon Snow's delicious fish salad.

2½ pounds	firm white fish fillets or steaks, such as halibut
	good olive oil
	kosher salt and freshly ground black pepper
½ cup	small-diced celery (2 stalks)
¾ cup	small-diced red onion
½ cup	small-diced fennel (optional)
½ cup	chopped fresh dill
¼ cup	freshly squeezed lemon juice (2 lemons)
¼ cup	good white wine vinegar
¼ cup	capers, drained
¾ cup	good mayonnaise

Preheat the oven to 400 degrees.

Place the fish on a sheet pan. Rub both sides with olive oil and sprinkle with salt and pepper. Roast for about 25 minutes, until the fish is firm and fully cooked. Allow to cool at room temperature for about 30 minutes. Remove and discard the skin and bones.

When the fish is cool, flake the meat into a bowl in large pieces. Add the celery, red onion, fennel (if using), dill, lemon juice, vinegar, capers, mayonnaise, 1 teaspoon salt, and ½ teaspoon pepper. Mix gently and refrigerate for 30 minutes. Taste for seasonings and serve at room temperature.

roasted shrimp & orzo

SERVES 6

This is a great summer lunch or dinner for a crowd. You can multiply the recipe to your heart's content. It's also great for parties because you can make it a day ahead of time. How easy is that?

Pasta cooked "al dente" literally means "to the tooth" in Italian. It's cooked through but has a slight resistance when you bite into it.

	kosher salt
	good olive oil
¾ pound	orzo (rice-shaped pasta)
½ cup	freshly squeezed lemon juice (3 lemons)
	freshly ground black pepper
2 pounds (16 to 18 count)	shrimp, peeled and deveined
1 cup	minced scallions, white and green parts
1 cup	chopped fresh dill
1 cup	chopped fresh flat-leaf parsley
1	hothouse cucumber, unpeeled, seeded, and medium-diced
½ cup	small-diced red onion
¾ pound	good feta cheese, large-diced

Preheat the oven to 400 degrees.

Fill a large pot with water, add 1 tablespoon salt and a splash of oil, and bring the water to a boil. Add the orzo and simmer for 9 to 11 minutes, stirring occasionally, until it's cooked al dente. Drain and pour into a large bowl. Whisk together the lemon juice, ½ cup olive oil, 2 teaspoons salt, and 1 teaspoon pepper. Pour over the hot pasta and stir well.

Meanwhile, place the shrimp on a sheet pan, drizzle with olive oil, and sprinkle with salt and pepper. Toss to combine and spread out in a single layer. Roast for 5 to 6 minutes, until the shrimp are cooked through. Don't overcook!

Add the shrimp to the orzo and then add the scallions, dill, parsley, cucumber, onion, 2 teaspoons salt, and 1 teaspoon pepper. Toss well. Add the feta and stir carefully. Set aside at room temperature for 1 hour to allow the flavors to blend, or refrigerate overnight. If refrigerated, taste again for seasonings and bring back to room temperature before serving.

pesto pea salad

SERVES 4 TO 6

In the summer when there's too much basil in my garden, I make lots of pesto. Pesto is an Italian basil and garlic sauce; it will keep for a week in the refrigerator and all winter in the freezer. This is a cold salad with pesto, but of course, pesto is also good on hot pasta for a quick dinner.

¼ pound	baby spinach leaves
1 (10-ounce) package	frozen peas, defrosted
½ cup	prepared pesto
¼ cup	freshly grated Parmesan cheese
1 teaspoon	kosher salt
2 tablespoons	toasted pine nuts (pignolis)

Wash the spinach leaves and spin them dry. Place the spinach and the peas in a large bowl. Add the pesto and Parmesan, then sprinkle with the salt. Toss well, sprinkle with pine nuts, and serve.

To toast pine nuts, place them in a dry sauté pan and cook them over medium-low heat, tossing frequently, for 5 to 10 minutes, until lightly browned.

If you want to make your own pesto, see Barefoot Contessa Parties.

warm duck salad

SERVES 4 TO 6

This is such a great summer lunch; it's substantial with the roast duck but also light and flavorful. This makes enough for four lunches or six appetizers. If you like something crunchy in the salad, you can make cracklings by roasting the fat and skin of the duck breasts at 400 degrees for twenty minutes and then dice it into the salad. Either way, it's just delicious. (For photograph, see page 60.)

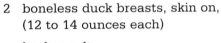

2	boneless duck breasts, skin on, (12 to 14 ounces each)
	kosher salt
1 tablespoon	minced shallots
2½ tablespoons	good sherry vinegar
1 teaspoon	grated orange zest
½ cup	good olive oil
3 heads	Belgian endive
3 ounces	mâche or other delicate baby lettuce
3	navel oranges, peeled, cut in half, and sliced
½ pint	fresh raspberries
1 cup	toasted whole pecan halves

To toast pecans, place them in a dry sauté pan and cook over medium-low heat for 5 to 10 minutes, tossing often to toast them evenly.

Preheat the oven to 400 degrees.

Place the duck breasts on a sheet pan, skin side up. Sprinkle with salt and roast for about 20 minutes, until medium-rare. Remove from the oven, cover tightly with aluminum foil, and allow to sit for 10 to 15 minutes. Remove and discard the fat and skin on top (unless you're making cracklings), slice the duck, and then cut the slices crosswise into julienne pieces.

Meanwhile, in a small bowl, combine the shallots, sherry vinegar, orange zest, and 1½ teaspoons of salt. Whisk in the olive oil and set aside.

For the salad, trim the bottom half-inch from the endives and cut them diagonally in $\frac{1}{2}$-inch slices. Separate the leaves and discard the cores. Place the slices in a large salad bowl. Add the mâche leaves, oranges, raspberries, and toasted pecans. Toss with enough of the dressing to moisten. Gently toss in the warm duck breasts and serve immediately.

tomato feta salad

SERVES 6

There are several kinds of feta available but I prefer Greek feta; it's a little dry and has lots of flavor. Bulgarian feta tends to be a bit saltier and French feta is milder, but they're all delicious, so you can certainly use whatever you like.

2 pints	cherry tomatoes, red or mixed colors
¾ cup	small-diced red onion
2 tablespoons	good white wine vinegar or champagne vinegar
3 tablespoons	good olive oil
1½ teaspoons	kosher salt
½ teaspoon	freshly ground black pepper
2 tablespoons	chopped fresh basil leaves
2 tablespoons	chopped fresh flat-leaf parsley
¾ pound	feta cheese

Cut the tomatoes in half and place them in a large bowl. Add the onion, vinegar, olive oil, salt, pepper, basil, and parsley and toss well. Dice the feta into a ½- to ¾-inch dice, crumbling it as little as possible. Gently fold it into the salad and serve at room temperature.

blue cheese coleslaw

SERVES 6 TO 8

I'm always looking for a way to give classic recipes a twist that gives them more flavor. My friend Antonia Bellanca took me to Fancy's, her favorite local specialty food store in Osterville, Massachusetts, and they offered a delicious blue cheese coleslaw. How bad could that be?

½ small head	green cabbage
½ small head	red cabbage
4 large	carrots
2 cups	good mayonnaise
¼ cup	Dijon mustard
2 tablespoons	whole-grain mustard
2 tablespoons	apple cider vinegar
1 teaspoon	celery salt
½ teaspoon	kosher salt
½ teaspoon	freshly ground black pepper
1½ cups	crumbled Roquefort (6 ounces)
1 cup	chopped fresh flat-leaf parsley

Cut the cabbage halves in half and cut out the cores. Set up the food processor with a slicing blade and place the pieces of cabbage horizontally into the feed tube, one at a time. (If they don't fit, cut them to fit lying down.) Insert the feed tube pusher and turn on the processor, but don't press on the feed tube pusher or the slices will turn out too thick! Continue with the remaining red and green cabbage. Transfer to a large bowl, discarding any very large pieces. Before you pour the dressing on the salad, save a handful of the grated vegetables to decorate for serving.

Change the slicing blade for a large shredding blade and cut the carrots so they will fit horizontally into the feed tube. Replace the feed tube pusher and press firmly with the food processor on. Transfer the shredded carrots to the bowl with the cabbages.

In a medium bowl, whisk together the mayonnaise, two mustards, vinegar, celery salt, kosher salt, and pepper. Pour enough mayonnaise dressing over the grated vegetables to moisten, and toss well. Add the Roquefort and the parsley and toss together. Cover the bowl with plastic wrap and refrigerate for several hours to allow the flavors to meld. Serve cold or at room temperature. Gernish with the reserved grated vegetables.

guacamole salad

SERVES 6

At Barefoot Contessa we just couldn't make enough guacamole to satisfy our customers. We used Hass avocados and just enough heat to make it interesting. So I thought, why couldn't I make a guacamole salad with all those wonderful flavors? Black beans add both color and texture.

1 pint	grape tomatoes, halved
1	yellow bell pepper, seeded and ½-inch diced
1 (15-ounce) can	black beans, rinsed and drained
½ cup	small-diced red onion
2 tablespoons	minced jalapeño peppers, seeded (2 peppers)
½ teaspoon	freshly grated lime zest
¼ cup	freshly squeezed lime juice (2 limes)
¼ cup	good olive oil
1 teaspoon	kosher salt
½ teaspoon	freshly ground black pepper
½ teaspoon	minced garlic
¼ teaspoon	ground cayenne pepper
2	ripe Hass avocados, seeded, peeled, and ½-inch diced

Place the tomatoes, yellow pepper, black beans, red onion, jalapeño peppers, and lime zest in a large bowl. Whisk together the lime juice, olive oil, salt, black pepper, garlic, and cayenne pepper and pour over the vegetables. Toss well.

Just before you're ready to serve the salad, fold the avocados into the salad. Check the seasoning and serve at room temperature.

old-fashioned potato salad

SERVES 6 TO 8

During the eighteen years that I owned Barefoot Contessa, we must have made millions of pounds of this classic potato salad. It's easy to make because you don't have to peel the potatoes.

3 pounds	small red potatoes
	kosher salt
1 cup	good mayonnaise
¼ cup	buttermilk, milk, or white wine
2 tablespoons	Dijon mustard
2 tablespoons	whole-grain mustard
½ cup	chopped fresh dill
	freshly ground black pepper
½ cup	medium-diced celery
½ cup	small-diced red onion

Allowing the potatoes to steam after you boil them results in evenly tender—but still firm—potatoes.

Place the potatoes and 2 tablespoons salt in a large pot of water. Bring the water to a boil, then lower the heat and simmer for 10 to 15 minutes, until the potatoes are barely tender when pierced with a knife. Drain the potatoes in a colander, then place the colander with the potatoes over the empty pot off the heat and cover with a clean, dry kitchen towel. Leave the potatoes to steam for 15 to 20 minutes, until tender but firm.

Meanwhile, in a small bowl, whisk together the mayonnaise, buttermilk, Dijon and whole-grain mustards, dill, 1 teaspoon salt, and 1 teaspoon pepper. Set aside.

When the potatoes are cool enough to handle, cut them into quarters or halves, depending on their size. Place the cut potatoes in a large bowl and pour enough dressing over them to moisten. (As the salad sits, you may need to add more dressing.) Add the celery and red onion, 2 teaspoons salt, and 1 teaspoon pepper. Toss well, cover, and refrigerate for a few hours to allow the flavors to blend.

dinner

blue cheese burgers

cornish hens with cornbread stuffing

chicken piccata

lamb kebabs with couscous

roast capon

loin of pork with fennel

stuffed cabbage

rib-eye steaks with
cornmeal-fried onion rings

portobello mushroom lasagna

chicken with goat cheese & basil

seafood gratin

eli's asian salmon

lemon fusilli with arugula

summer garden pasta

seared tuna with mango chutney

easy lobster paella

the important dinner

I recently found myself at a party seated next to the CEO of a major international corporation. After I got over my initial panic about finding a topic of conversation, we started talking about dinner parties in general. He told me that he felt the worst parties were those given by the people who work for him because the hosts were always trying so hard to impress. It made him uncomfortable that not only did they seem to spend their annual salaries on the dinner, which I can understand would be really embarrassing, but also they're always apologizing for everything. "I'm sorry the children are so noisy, I'm sorry, the soup's too cold." "I have children," he told me, "I know they're noisy." At the end of the day, everyone—even the CEO of a major international corporation—just wants a simple, delicious meal and a good conversation with friends. For me, this kind of occasion calls for a well-planned menu, something really comforting and not pretentious that's ready before the guests arrive.

I would start by basing the menu on things I really—*really*—know how to make. This isn't the time to test that intriguing recipe from the latest *Gourmet*; this is the time for something tried-and-true that you know will make people smile. In the winter I might make a roasted capon with carrots and potatoes that I'll carve at the

table. For a summer dinner, I would make Eli's Asian salmon with garlic and herb tomatoes and a dramatic berry Pavlova—meringue, whipped cream, and berries—for dessert. Familiar food relaxes everyone, especially the host.

I'd also only serve things that I could make in advance. I've said this so many times before but it's really worth repeating: there's no substitute for the host actually being present at a party. No matter how much time you spend making dinner, your guests would really rather believe that you whipped it up in the few minutes before they arrived. Making a complicated, expensive dinner doesn't flatter them *nearly* as much as spending the evening talking to them. Ask them lots of questions about themselves and they'll think you're the most interesting person in the room.

Once you've got the menu and the timing under control, give yourself a break. The best parties are the ones where the host and hostess are having fun, so relax, pour yourself a glass of wine, and enjoy your own party. Your important guests will pick up on your party spirit and have a good time, too. And instead of the formal dinners they usually have to endure, they'll be thrilled to be spending the evening with someone who has enough confidence to serve a simple, delicious roast chicken for dinner. Wouldn't you?

blue cheese burgers

MAKES 8 TO 10 BURGERS

While you can certainly make these as plain hamburgers—and they're delicious!—blue cheese just takes them to the next level. Allowing the hamburgers to "rest" the way you do a grilled steak makes them particularly juicy.

2 pounds	ground chuck
1 pound	ground sirloin
3 tablespoons	Crosse & Blackwell steak sauce
6	extra-large egg yolks
1½ teaspoons	kosher salt
¾ teaspoon	freshly ground black pepper
4 tablespoons (½ stick)	cold unsalted butter
8 to 10	hamburger buns
8 ounces	blue cheese, such as Danish Blue
	arugula, for serving
	sliced tomatoes, for serving

If you want delicious brioche hamburger buns, you can order them by mail from www.elizabar.com. Otherwise, Pepperidge Farm makes very good hamburger buns.

In a large bowl, carefully mix the meats, steak sauce, egg yolks, salt, and pepper with the tines of a fork, but do not mash the mixture. Lightly form hamburger patties and press lightly into shape. Press a thin slice of butter into the top of each hamburger, making sure the meat entirely encases the butter.

Prepare a charcoal or a stovetop grill and cook the hamburgers for 4 minutes on one side, turn, and cook for 3 minutes on the other side for medium-rare. Remove to a plate and cover with aluminum foil. Allow the hamburgers to rest for 5 minutes. Meanwhile, grill the buns, cut side down, for 1 minute, until toasted. Place a hamburger and a slice of blue cheese on each bun, plus arugula and tomato and serve hot.

cornish hens with cornbread stuffing

SERVES 6

Sick of turkey for Thanksgiving? I like to shake up tradition and give everyone their own little bird stuffed with moist, delicious cornbread stuffing. You can make the cornbread from scratch (see page 154) or buy some at a bakery. This is also an easy dinner to make for a party.

For the stuffing

¼ pound (1 stick)	unsalted butter
1 cup	chopped yellow onion
1½ cups	medium-diced celery (3 stalks)
3 tablespoons	chopped fresh flat-leaf parsley
5 cups (13 ounces)	coarsely crumbled cornbread
½ cup	chicken stock, preferably homemade (page 45)

For the hens

6	fresh Cornish hens (1¼- to 1½-pounds)
2 cups	sliced yellow onions (2 onions)
	kosher salt and freshly ground black pepper
2 tablespoons	unsalted butter, melted

Preheat the oven to 400 degrees.

For the stuffing, melt the butter in a medium sauté pan, add the onion, and cook over medium-low heat for 8 minutes, until translucent. Off the heat, add the celery, parsley, cornbread, and chicken stock and mix well. Set aside.

For the hens, rinse them inside and out, removing any pin feathers, and pat the outsides dry. In a roasting pan that's just large enough to hold the hens loosely, first toss in the onions and then place the hens on top, breast side up. Sprinkle the insides of the hens with salt and pepper and loosely fill the cavities with the stuffing. (If there is stuffing left over, bake it in a separate pan until heated through.) Tie the legs of each hen together and tuck the wings under the bodies. Brush with melted butter, sprinkle with salt and pepper, and roast for 50 to 60 minutes, until the skin is browned and the juices run clear when you cut between a leg and thigh. Remove from the oven, cover with aluminum foil, and allow to rest for 15 minutes. Serve a whole hen per person.

chicken piccata

SERVES 4

One of my favorite restaurants in East Hampton is The Palm and I always order the veal piccata. I thought it would be great if I could whip up a chicken piccata for a quick dinner. Once I got the system down for the sauce, I made this over and over again.

4 split (2 whole)	boneless, skinless chicken breasts
	kosher salt and freshly ground black pepper
1 cup	all-purpose flour
2	extra-large eggs
1½ cups	seasoned dried bread crumbs
	good olive oil
3 tablespoons	unsalted butter, at room temperature
⅓ cup	freshly squeezed lemon juice (2 lemons), lemon halves reserved
½ cup	dry white wine
	sliced lemon, for serving
	chopped fresh flat-leaf parsley, for serving

Preheat the oven to 400 degrees. Line a sheet pan with parchment paper.

Place each chicken breast between 2 sheets of parchment paper or plastic wrap and pound it out to ¼-inch thick. Sprinkle both sides with salt and pepper.

Mix the flour, 1 teaspoon salt, and ½ teaspoon pepper on a shallow plate. In a second plate, beat the eggs and 1 tablespoon water together. Place the bread crumbs on a third plate. Dip each chicken breast first in the flour, shake off the excess, and then dip in the egg and bread-crumb mixtures.

Heat 2 tablespoons olive oil in a large sauté pan over medium to medium-low heat. Add 2 chicken breasts and cook for 2 minutes on each side, until browned. Place them on the sheet pan while you cook the rest of the chicken. Heat more olive oil in the sauté pan and cook the second 2 chicken breasts. Place them on the same sheet pan and allow them to bake for 5 to 10 minutes while you make the sauce.

For the sauce, wipe out the sauté pan with a dry paper towel. On medium heat, melt 1 tablespoon of the butter and then add the lemon juice, white wine, the reserved lemon halves, ½ teaspoon salt, and ¼ teaspoon pepper. Boil over high heat until reduced by half, about 2 minutes. Off the heat, add the remaining 2 tablespoons of butter and swirl to combine. Discard the lemon halves. Serve one chicken breast on each plate, spoon on the sauce, and serve with sliced lemon and a sprinkling of fresh parsley.

lamb kebabs
with couscous

SERVES 4 TO 6

I'm always looking for a special dinner that's quick. I marinate the lamb a day or two in advance and then all I have to do is grill skewers of lamb and cherry tomatoes and make the couscous, which is so easy. This couscous recipe is from my friend Anna Pump's Loaves & Fishes cookbook. For the marinade, use the same dry red wine that you're going to serve with dinner, such as an Italian Chianti.

2 pounds	top round lamb
1 tablespoon	minced garlic (2 to 3 cloves)
1 tablespoon	minced fresh rosemary leaves
2 teaspoons	minced fresh thyme leaves
	good olive oil
¼ cup	dry red wine
2 tablespoons	red wine vinegar
	kosher salt and freshly ground black pepper
2 to 3 small	red onions
2 pints	cherry tomatoes

For the sauce

½ cup	good chicken stock, preferably homemade (page 45)
¼ cup	good olive oil
1 tablespoon	freshly squeezed lemon juice
	pinch of minced fresh rosemary leaves
¼ teaspoon	kosher salt
¼ teaspoon	freshly ground black pepper
	Couscous with Pine Nuts, for serving (recipe follows)

Cut the lamb into 1½-inch cubes. You should have about 20 cubes. Combine the garlic, rosemary, thyme, ¼ cup olive oil, red wine, vinegar, and 1 teaspoon salt in a medium bowl. Add the lamb cubes, cover with plastic wrap, and refrigerate overnight or for up to 2 days. Toss occasionally.

Heat a grill with coals. Spread them out in one dense layer and brush the grill with oil.

Cut the red onions into quarters and separate each quarter into 3 or 4 sections. Loosely thread 3 or 4 pieces of lamb onto skewers alternately with sections of onion. Sprinkle both sides of the lamb with salt and pepper. Next place the cherry tomatoes on skewers, threading them through the stems of the tomatoes. Brush the tomatoes with olive oil and sprinkle with salt and pepper. Place the lamb skewers on the hot grill and cook for 10 to 15 minutes, turning 2 or 3 times, until the lamb is medium-rare. Approximately 5 minutes before the lamb is done, place the tomato skewers on the grill, turning once, until seared on the outside but still firm inside.

For the sauce, bring the chicken stock, olive oil, and lemon juice to a boil in a small pot. Lower the heat and simmer for 5 minutes, or until reduced by half. Add the rosemary, salt, and pepper.

Serve the skewers on a mound of couscous with the sauce on the side.

couscous with pine nuts

SERVES 4 TO 6

4 tablespoons (½ stick)	unsalted butter
¾ cup	chopped shallots (3 to 4 shallots)
3 cups	chicken stock, preferably homemade (page 45)
½ teaspoon	kosher salt
½ teaspoon	freshly ground black pepper
1½ cups	couscous
½ cup	toasted pine nuts (pignolis)
¼ cup	dried currants
2 tablespoons	chopped fresh flat-leaf parsley

Melt the butter in a large saucepan. Add the shallots and cook them over medium-low heat for 3 minutes, until translucent. Add the chicken stock, salt, and pepper and bring to a boil. Turn off the heat. Stir in the couscous, cover the pan, and set aside for 10 minutes. Add the pine nuts, currants, and parsley and fluff with a fork to combine. Serve hot.

Israeli—or pearl—couscous has larger grains and cooks differently, so don't use it for this recipe.

To toast pine nuts, put them in a dry sauté pan over medium heat, tossing often, for 5 to 10 minutes, until lightly browned.

roast capon

SERVES 6

Capon is rooster that's been—how shall I say this delicately?—"altered" to become a hen. They tend to grow much larger than chickens—about eight to ten pounds—so they're a terrific alternative for a holiday . . . or if you're just having a few friends in for a simple dinner.

1 (8- to 10-pound)	fresh capon
	kosher salt and freshly ground black pepper
2	lemons, quartered
12	sprigs fresh thyme
4 tablespoons (½ stick)	unsalted butter, melted
2	yellow onions, sliced
2 pounds	carrots cut diagonally into 2-inch chunks

When you bring the capon home, sprinkle the outside of the bird liberally with salt. Wrap it well and refrigerate until you are ready to roast it. The capon can sit in the refrigerator for up to 2 days.

Preheat the oven to 425 degrees.

Place the capon, breast side up, in a large (13 × 16 × 3-inch) roasting pan and pat the outside dry with paper towels. Sprinkle the cavity generously with salt and pepper. Place the lemons and thyme inside the cavity. Tie the legs together with kitchen string and tie the wings close to the body of the capon. Brush the capon with half of the melted butter, then sprinkle with 1 tablespoon salt and 1 teaspoon pepper. Place the onions and carrots in a large bowl. Add the rest of the melted butter to the onion and carrot mixture plus another 1 tablespoon salt and 1 teaspoon pepper and toss well. Place the onions and carrots around the capon. Place the capon into the oven legs first (the back of the oven tends to be hotter than the front) and roast for 1½ hours, until the juices run clear when you cut between the leg and the thigh.

Remove the capon from the oven and cover the pan with aluminum foil. (If the vegetables aren't browned, transfer the capon to a platter and cover with aluminum foil. Return the vegetables to the oven to cook while the meat rests.) Allow the capon to rest for 20 minutes, then carve it and serve warm with the vegetables. Skim the fat off the pan juices and pour over the carved capon and vegetables.

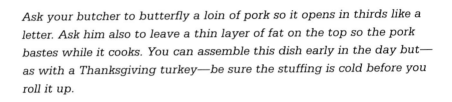

loin of pork with fennel

SERVES 6

Ask your butcher to butterfly a loin of pork so it opens in thirds like a letter. Ask him also to leave a thin layer of fat on the top so the pork bastes while it cooks. You can assemble this dish early in the day but— as with a Thanksgiving turkey—be sure the stuffing is cold before you roll it up.

For fresh bread crumbs, remove the crusts of white sandwich bread, cut the slices in large cubes, and process in the bowl of a food processor fitted with steel blade. Depending on which bread you choose, you'll need 6 to 12 slices.

	good olive oil
1 tablespoon	unsalted butter
2 cups	sliced yellow onions (2 onions)
2 cups	sliced fennel (1 large bulb)
	kosher salt
	freshly ground black pepper
2 teaspoons	minced garlic (2 large cloves)
1 tablespoon	minced fresh thyme leaves
1 tablespoon	Pernod or white wine
3 cups	fresh bread crumbs
1 (3½-pound)	loin of pork, butterflied (see above)

Preheat the oven to 425 degrees.

For the stuffing, heat 1 tablespoon of olive oil and the butter in a large (12-inch) sauté pan. Add the onions and fennel with 1 teaspoon salt and ½ teaspoon pepper. Cook over low to medium-low heat for 15 minutes, stirring occasionally, until the onions and fennel are tender and lightly browned. Add the garlic and thyme and cook for 1 more minute. Add the Pernod and cook for 1 more minute, deglazing the pan. Cool slightly.

Add the bread crumbs and 1 teaspoon of salt to the stuffing mixture. Lay the pork on a board, fat side down, and sprinkle with salt and pepper. Spread the stuffing evenly on the pork and roll up lengthwise, ending with the fat on the top of the roll. Tie with kitchen string, rub with olive oil, and sprinkle liberally with salt and pepper.

Place the rolled pork loin on a baking rack on a sheet pan and roast for 30 minutes. Lower the heat to 350 degrees and roast for another 20 to 30 minutes, until the interior of the pork is 137 degrees. (If the thermometer hits stuffing rather than pork, it will register a higher temperature, so test the meat in several places.) Remove from the oven and cover tightly with aluminum foil. Allow to rest for 15 minutes. Remove the strings, slice thickly, and serve.

stuffed cabbage

SERVES 6

This is old-fashioned Jewish peasant food and it's so good on a cold winter night. To some it's an acquired taste, but it's a very inexpensive and satisfying dinner. I think children love the fact that they can have raisins in their dinner.

3 tablespoons	good olive oil
1½ cups	chopped yellows onions (2 onions)
2 (28-ounce) cans	crushed tomatoes and their juice
¼ cup	red wine vinegar
½ cup	light brown sugar, lightly packed
½ cup	raisins
1½ teaspoons	kosher salt
¾ teaspoon	freshly ground black pepper
1 large head	Savoy or green cabbage, including outer leaves

For the filling

2½ pounds	ground chuck
3	extra-large eggs, lightly beaten
½ cup	finely chopped yellow onion
½ cup	plain dried bread crumbs
½ cup	uncooked white rice
1 teaspoon	minced fresh thyme leaves
1½ teaspoons	kosher salt
½ teaspoon	freshly ground black pepper

For the sauce, heat the olive oil in a large saucepan, add the onions, and cook over medium-low heat for 8 minutes, until the onions are translucent. Add the tomatoes, vinegar, brown sugar, raisins, salt, and pepper. Bring to a boil, then lower the heat and simmer uncovered for 30 minutes, stirring occasionally. Set aside.

Meanwhile, bring a large pot of water to a boil.

Remove the *entire* core of the cabbage with a paring knife. Immerse the head of cabbage in the boiling water for a few minutes, peeling off each leaf with tongs as soon as it's flexible. Set the leaves aside. Depending on the size of each leaf, you will need at least 14 leaves.

For the filling, in a large bowl, combine the ground chuck, eggs, onion, bread crumbs, rice, thyme, salt, and pepper. Add 1 cup of the sauce to the meat mixture and mix lightly with a fork.

Preheat the oven to 350 degrees.

To assemble, place 1 cup of the sauce in the bottom of a large Dutch oven. Remove the hard triangular rib from the base of each cabbage leaf with a small paring knife. Place ⅓ to ½ cup of filling in an oval shape near the rib edge of each leaf and roll up toward the outer edge, tucking the sides in as you roll. Place half the cabbage rolls, seam sides down, over the sauce. Add more sauce and more cabbage rolls alternately until you've placed all the cabbage rolls in the pot. Pour the remaining sauce over the cabbage rolls. Cover the dish tightly with the lid and bake for 1 hour, or until the meat is cooked and the rice is tender. Serve hot.

rib-eye steaks with cornmeal-fried onion rings

SERVES 4 TO 6

Whenever I go to the butcher for steaks, I'm stumped about which cut is best. To settle it once and for all, Jeffrey and I decided to grill three different cuts one summer day and it became absolutely clear which one we liked best. New York strip steak is also called shell steak or Kansas City strip, and filet mignon is a cross-cut slice from a whole filet of beef. They're both great, but our favorite was the rib-eye steak, a slice of a standing rib roast. If you can find aged steaks, such as those from Niman Ranch, they're particularly tender and flavorful.

For 1½-inch steaks, sear them for 2 minutes on each side and then cook them for 4 to 6 minutes, until the internal temperature reaches 120 degrees. Allow to rest before serving.

4 (1¼-inch thick)   rib-eye steaks, either boneless or bone in
kosher salt and freshly ground black pepper
good olive oil
Cornmeal-Fried Onion Rings (recipe follows)

Thirty minutes before grilling the steaks, remove them from the refrigerator and allow them to come to room temperature. Heat a grill with coals.

When the coals are hot, spread them out in the grill in one solid layer. Pat the steaks dry on both sides with paper towels and sprinkle them liberally with salt and pepper. Place the steaks on the hot grill and sear them on each side for 2 minutes, until browned. Brush each side lightly with olive oil. Place the lid on the grill and allow the steaks to cook for another 3 to 4 minutes, until they are cooked rare, or 120 degrees on a meat thermometer. (To test the steaks, insert the thermometer sideways to be sure you're actually testing the middle of the steak.) Remove the steaks from the grill, place them in one layer on a platter, and cover tightly with aluminum foil. Allow the steaks to rest at room temperature for 15 minutes. Slice and serve warm with the cornmeal-fried onion rings.

cornmeal-fried onion rings

SERVES 4 TO 6

I love old-fashioned onion rings but I always thought they were impossible to make. I came up with this easy recipe and discovered that if you use a large pot rather than a frying pan, you won't end up with grease all over the kitchen. Serve these on top of the rib-eye steak and your friends will go crazy.

2 large	Spanish onions (or 3 yellow onions)
2 cups	buttermilk
	kosher salt and freshly ground black pepper
1½ cups	all-purpose flour
¼ cup	(medium) yellow cornmeal
1 quart	vegetable oil

Peel the onions, slice them ½- to ¾-inch thick, and separate them into rings. Combine the buttermilk, 1½ teaspoons salt, and 1 teaspoon pepper in a medium bowl. Add the onion rings, toss well, and allow to marinate for at least 15 minutes. (The onion rings can sit in the buttermilk for a few hours.) In a separate bowl, combine the flour, cornmeal, 1 teaspoon salt, and ½ teaspoon pepper. Set aside.

When you're ready to fry the onion rings, preheat the oven to 200 degrees. Line a baking sheet with paper towels.

Heat the oil to 350 degrees in a large pot or Dutch oven. (A candy thermometer attached to the side of the pot will help you maintain the proper temperature.) Working in batches, lift some onions out of the buttermilk and dredge them in the flour mixture. Drop into the hot oil and fry for 2 minutes, until golden brown, turning them once with tongs. Don't crowd them! Place the finished onion rings on the baking sheet, sprinkle liberally with salt, and keep them warm in the oven while you fry the next batches. Continue frying the onion rings and placing them in the warm oven until all the onions are fried. They will remain crisp in the oven for up to 30 minutes. Serve hot.

portobello mushroom lasagna

SERVES 6

Lasagna is classically an Italian dish, but it's also commonly made in Provence. The French somehow make it a little more elegant. Portobello mushrooms have so much more flavor than our traditional "button" mushrooms that they can stand alone in a simple pasta. This is a good substantial meal for a vegetarian but can also be served as a side dish with a roast.

To make this ahead, assemble the lasagna and keep it refrigerated until ready to serve. Bake for an additional 10 minutes, until browned and bubbly.

	kosher salt
	good olive oil
¾ pound	dried lasagna noodles
4 cups	whole milk
12 tablespoons (1½ sticks)	unsalted butter, divided
½ cup	all-purpose flour
1 teaspoon	freshly ground black pepper
1 teaspoon	ground nutmeg
1½ pounds	portobello mushrooms
1 cup	freshly grated Parmesan cheese

Preheat the oven to 375 degrees.

Bring a large pot of water to a boil with 1 tablespoon salt and a splash of oil. Add the lasagna noodles and cook for 10 minutes, stirring occasionally. Drain and set aside.

For the white sauce, bring the milk to a simmer in a saucepan. Set aside. Melt 8 tablespoons (1 stick) of the butter in a large saucepan. Add the flour and cook for 1 minute over low heat, stirring constantly with a wooden spoon. Pour the hot milk into the butter-flour mixture all at once. Add 1 tablespoon salt, the pepper, and nutmeg, and cook over medium-low heat, stirring first with the wooden spoon and then with a whisk, for 3 to 5 minutes, until thick. Set aside off the heat.

Separate the mushroom stems from the caps and discard the stems. Slice the caps ¼-inch thick. Heat 2 tablespoons of oil and 2 tablespoons of the butter in a large (12-inch) sauté pan. When the butter melts, add half the mushrooms, sprinkle with salt, and cook over medium heat for about 5 minutes, until the mushrooms are tender and they release some of their juices. If they become too dry, add a little more oil. Toss occasionally to make sure the mushrooms cook evenly. Repeat with the remaining mushrooms and set all the mushrooms aside.

To assemble the lasagna, spread some of the sauce in the bottom of an 8 × 12 × 2-inch baking dish. Arrange a layer of noodles on top, then more sauce, then one-third of the mushrooms, and ¼ cup grated Parmesan cheese. Repeat two more times, layering noodles, sauce, mushrooms, and Parmesan. Top with a final layer of noodles and sauce, and sprinkle with the remaining Parmesan.

Bake the lasagna for 45 minutes, or until the top is browned and the sauce is bubbly and hot. Allow to sit at room temperature for 15 minutes and serve hot.

chicken with goat cheese & basil

SERVES 4 TO 6

Everyone needs a few dishes they can assemble ten minutes after they walk in the door at night. When I'm too tired to cook and really want a hot meal, this is my first choice. If you can't find garlic-and-herb Montrachet, it's also good with any plain, creamy goat cheese.

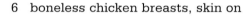

6	boneless chicken breasts, skin on
8 to 10 ounces	garlic-and-herb goat cheese, such as Montrachet
6 large	fresh basil leaves
	good olive oil
	kosher salt and freshly ground black pepper

Preheat the oven to 375 degrees.

Place the chicken breasts on a sheet pan. Loosen the skin from the meat with your fingers, leaving one side attached. Cut the goat cheese into ½-inch-thick slices and place 1 or 2 slices plus a large basil leaf under the skin of each chicken breast. Pull the skin over as much of the meat as possible so the chicken won't dry out. With your fingers, rub each piece with olive oil, then sprinkle them very generously with salt and pepper. Bake the chicken for 35 to 40 minutes, until the skin is lightly browned and the chicken is just cooked through. Serve hot or at room temperature.

You might have to ask your butcher for boneless chicken breasts with the skin on.

To make this ahead, assemble the chicken breasts and refrigerate. Bake just before serving.

seafood gratin

SERVES 4

I love lobster Newburg, but these days it's a little too rich for my taste. This seafood gratin has a light saffron sauce and can be assembled early and baked before dinner. Panko are Japanese bread crumbs; they're now quite widely available in the Asian section of many grocery stores as well as in seafood shops. The panko and Parmesan crust gives the gratin a really flavorful crunch.

1 cup	seafood stock (page 55) or clam juice
1 cup	heavy cream
½ cup plus 3 tablespoons	good white wine, such as Chablis
3 tablespoons	tomato purée
½ teaspoon	saffron threads
8 ounces	raw shrimp, peeled, deveined, and cut in half crosswise
8 ounces	raw halibut, cut into 1-inch chunks
8 ounces	cooked lobster meat, cut into 1-inch chunks
7 tablespoons	unsalted butter, divided
1 tablespoon	all-purpose flour
	kosher salt and freshly ground black pepper
3 cups	julienned leeks, white and light green parts (2 large)
1½ cups	julienned carrots (3 carrots)
1 cup	panko (Japanese dried bread crumbs)
⅓ cup	freshly grated Parmesan cheese
2 tablespoons	minced fresh flat-leaf parsley
1 tablespoon	chopped fresh tarragon leaves
1 tablespoon	minced garlic (2 cloves)

To julienne leeks, wash them thoroughly and cut lengthwise into ½-inch strips. Cut crosswise into 2-inch pieces. For the carrots, peel them, cut into ¼-inch strips, and cut into 2-inch pieces.

Preheat the oven to 375 degrees. Place 4 individual gratin dishes on sheet pans.

For the sauce, combine the stock, cream, ½ cup of the wine, the tomato purée, and saffron in a medium saucepan. Bring to a boil, lower the heat, and add the shrimp. After 3 minutes, use a

slotted spoon to remove the shrimp to a bowl. Add the halibut
to the stock for about 3 minutes, until just cooked through, and
remove to the same bowl. Add the cooked lobster to the bowl.

Continue to cook the sauce until reduced by half, about
12 minutes. Mash 1 tablespooon of the butter together with
the flour. Whisk the butter mixture into the sauce along with
1 teaspoon salt and ½ teaspoon pepper. Simmer, stirring constantly, until thickened, about 5 minutes. Set aside.

Melt 3 tablespoons of the butter in a medium sauté pan.
Add the leeks and carrots and cook over medium heat for 5 minutes, until softened. Add the remaining 3 tablespoons of wine, ½
teaspoon salt, and ¼ teaspoon pepper and cook for 5 to 10 minutes, until tender. Set aside.

Combine the panko, Parmesan, parsley, tarragon, and garlic.
Melt the remaining 3 tablespoons of butter and mix it into the
crumbs until they're
moistened.

Divide the seafood
among the 4 gratin
dishes. Strew the
vegetables on top of
each dish. Pour the
sauce equally over
the seafood and veg-
etables and spoon the
crumbs evenly on top.
Bake for 20 minutes,
until the top is
browned and the
sauce is bubbly.
Serve hot.

eli's asian salmon

SERVES 5

This amazing recipe comes from Keith Eldridge, who is the executive chef for Eli Zabar at Eli's Manhattan, The Vinegar Factory, and E.A.T., all in New York City. I can't go into any of those stores without buying a piece of this salmon, and I was thrilled that they were willing to share the recipe with me. It's great hot, but in the summer it's also delicious at room temperature. Keith uses grated focaccia crumbs, made in a food processor with the grating disk, to top the fish, but panko is a good substitute. You will find many of these ingredients at Asian grocery stores and some supermarkets.

2¼ pounds	center-cut salmon fillet (1½ inches thick)
1 cup	soy sauce
¼ cup	rice vinegar
¼ cup	freshly squeezed lemon juice (2 lemons)
2 tablespoons	oyster sauce
1 tablespoon	fish sauce
1 tablespoon	toasted (dark) sesame oil
1½ teaspoons	chili paste
½ cup	sliced scallions (2 scallions)
2 tablespoons	minced garlic (8 large cloves)
2 tablespoons	minced fresh ginger
1½ cups	panko (Japanese bread crumbs)

I use Kikkoman soy sauce.

Be sure your oven is absolutely clean before you turn it to 500 degrees.

Line an 8 × 12-inch baking pan with aluminum foil. Place the salmon in the pan.

In a mixing cup, combine the soy sauce, rice vinegar, lemon juice, oyster sauce, fish sauce, sesame oil, chili paste, scallions, garlic, and ginger. Pour one-third of the soy sauce mixture over the salmon fillet. Sprinkle the panko evenly over the fillet. Pour the rest of the soy sauce mixture evenly over the panko. Be sure to soak the panko completely and if any run off, spoon them back onto the salmon. Set aside for 15 minutes, leaving all the sauce in the pan.

Meanwhile, preheat the oven to 500 degrees. Roast the salmon for 18 to 20 minutes, or for about 12 minutes per inch at the thickest part of the salmon. The internal temperature should be 120 degrees on a meat thermometer when it's done. Remove from the oven, wrap tightly with aluminum foil, and allow to rest for 15 minutes. Serve hot or at room temperature.

lemon fusilli
with arugula

SERVES 4 TO 5

This is a tried-and-true Barefoot Contessa recipe. Whenever we were running out of dinners, it was something quick we could whip up in large quantities with whatever fresh vegetables we had around. It's also a great last-minute dinner; I make a lot and then reheat just enough for dinner all week long.

1 tablespoon	good olive oil
1 tablespoon	minced garlic (2 cloves)
2 cups	heavy cream
3	lemons
	kosher salt and freshly ground black pepper
1 pound	dried fusilli pasta
½ pound	baby arugula (or 2 bunches of regular arugula, stems removed and leaves cut into thirds)
½ cup	freshly grated Parmesan cheese
1 pint	grape or cherry tomatoes, halved

Heat the olive oil in a medium saucepan over medium heat. Add the garlic, and cook for 60 seconds, then add the cream, the zest and juice of 2 of the lemons, 2 teaspoons salt, and 1 teaspoon pepper. Bring to a boil, then lower the heat and simmer for 15 to 20 minutes, until it starts to thicken.

Bring a large pot of water to a boil, add 1 tablespoon salt and the pasta, and cook al dente according to the directions on the package, about 12 minutes, stirring occasionally. Drain the pasta and return it to the pot. Immediately add the cream mixture and cook over medium-low heat for 3 minutes, until the pasta has absorbed most of the sauce. Pour the hot pasta into a large bowl and add the arugula, Parmesan, and tomatoes. Cut the last lemon in half lengthwise, slice it ¼-inch thick crosswise, and add a few slices to the pasta. Toss well, season to taste, and serve hot.

summer garden pasta

SERVES 6

This is a recipe from my friend Jean Halberstam, who had a wonderful cookware store in Nantucket and is also a renowned cook. This recipe uses surprisingly simple ingredients but it has lots of flavor without being loaded with butter and cream. It's the essence of summer. Jean says her husband, David, calls it a "three-bowler."

4 pints	cherry tomatoes, halved
	good olive oil
2 tablespoons	minced garlic (6 cloves)
18 large	basil leaves, julienned, plus extra for serving
½ teaspoon	crushed red pepper flakes
	kosher salt
½ teaspoon	freshly ground black pepper
1 pound	dried angel hair pasta
1½ cups	freshly grated Parmesan cheese, plus extra for serving

Grate the Parmesan cheese by cutting off the rind, cutting it into chunks, and processing it in a food processor fitted with a steel blade. It's really ground rather than grated.

Combine the cherry tomatoes, ½ cup olive oil, garlic, basil leaves, red pepper flakes, 1 teaspoon salt, and the pepper in a large bowl. Cover with plastic wrap, and set aside at room temperature for about 4 hours.

Just before you're ready to serve, bring a large pot of water with a splash of olive oil and 2 tablespoons salt to a boil and add the pasta. Cook al dente according to the directions on the package (be careful—it only takes 2 to 3 minutes!). Drain the pasta well and add to the bowl with the cherry tomatoes. Add the cheese and some extra fresh basil leaves and toss well. Serve in big bowls with extra cheese on each serving.

seared tuna with mango chutney

SERVES 4 TO 6

When fresh tuna is overcooked, it gets really dry and flavorless. To make sure that doesn't happen, I like to cook it in a very hot sauté pan or grill it over hot coals, until the outside is seared and the inside is raw, like sushi. The mango chutney is the perfect accompaniment.

	good olive oil
1 cup	chopped yellow onion
2 tablespoons	minced fresh ginger
2 cups	large-diced fresh mango (1 or 2 mangoes)
¼ cup	freshly squeezed orange juice
2 tablespoons	cider vinegar
¼ cup	golden raisins
¼ cup	sugar
	kosher salt
2 to 3 pounds	center-cut fresh tuna steak (1 inch thick)
	freshly ground black pepper

For the chutney, heat 2 tablespoons olive oil in a medium sauté pan. Add the onion and ginger and cook over medium-low heat for 5 to 10 minutes, until the onion is tender. Lower the heat, add the mango, and cook over low heat for 5 minutes, stirring occasionally. Add the orange juice, cider vinegar, raisins, sugar, and ½ teaspoon salt and cook over medium-low heat for 10 to 15 minutes, until the liquid is reduced.

Meanwhile, for the tuna, preheat a large, dry sauté pan (or 2 medium pans) over medium-high heat for 2 to 3 minutes, until very hot. Rub both sides of the tuna with olive oil and sprinkle with salt and pepper. When the pan is hot, place the tuna in the pan and cook for just 2 to 3 minutes on each side, until browned on the outside but still raw inside. Slice the tuna steaks thickly across the grain and serve with the mango chutney.

easy lobster paella

SERVES 6

Paella was a dish I made a lot in the 1970s but there were so many parts to it—the chicken, the sausage, the shellfish, the rice—that it was always a major production. Since Jeffrey loves it, I decided to find a way to make an elegant paella dinner that didn't take forever to prepare. I buy cooked lobster meat at the seafood shop, but you can certainly cook two lobsters yourself.

¼ cup	good olive oil
1½ cups	chopped yellow onions (2 onions)
2	red bell peppers, cored and sliced into ½-inch strips
2 tablespoons	minced garlic (4 to 6 cloves)
2 cups	white basmati rice
5 cups	good chicken stock, preferably homemade (page 45)
½ teaspoon	saffron threads, crushed
¼ teaspoon	crushed red pepper flakes
1 tablespoon	kosher salt
1 teaspoon	freshly ground black pepper
⅓ cup	Pernod
1½ pounds	cooked lobster meat
1 pound	kielbasa, sliced ¼- to ½-inch thick
1 (10-ounce) package	frozen peas
1 tablespoon	minced fresh flat-leaf parsley
2	lemons, cut into wedges

Traditionally, paella is made with chorizo, which needs to be cooked. I use kielbasa, which is precooked.

Preheat the oven to 425 degrees.

Heat the oil in a large ovenproof Dutch oven. Add the onions and cook over medium-low heat for 5 minutes, stirring occasionally. Add the bell peppers and cook over medium heat for 5 more minutes. Lower the heat, add the garlic, and cook for 1 minute longer. Stir in the rice, chicken stock, saffron, red pepper flakes, salt, and pepper and bring to a boil. Cover the pot and place it in the oven. After 15 minutes, stir the rice gently with a wooden spoon, and return it to the oven to bake uncovered for 10 to 15 more minutes, until the rice is fully cooked.

Transfer the paella back to the stove top and add the Pernod. Cook the paella over medium heat for 1 minute, until the Pernod is absorbed by the rice. Turn off the heat and add the lobster, kielbasa, and peas and stir gently. Cover the paella, and allow it to steam for 10 minutes. Sprinkle with the parsley, garnish with lemon wedges, and serve hot.

vegetables

garlic & herb tomatoes

orange-honey glazed carrots

broccolini & balsamic vinaigrette

zucchini pancakes

herbed basmati rice

green green spring vegetables

buttermilk mashed potatoes

stewed lentils & tomatoes

parmesan-roasted cauliflower

creamy rosemary polenta

broccoli rabe with garlic

maple baked beans

mustard-roasted potatoes

jalapeño cheddar cornbread

herb-roasted onions

planning a menu

One of the questions I'm often asked is, "Can you put a menu together for me?" It's usually for a special occasion or a holiday, but frankly, I think menu planning is a challenge at any time. I've been doing it for so long for myself and for catering clients, so I finally sat down and thought about how I do it. I realized that it's really a multipart decision. Here is what I think about:

First, I figure out what kind of event the meal is. Is it an occasion that requires a special menu? Roast chicken on the first New Year's Eve of the millennium just wouldn't do, but by the same token fettuccine with truffles feels too pretentious for a family dinner. Events honoring someone make me want to cook the person's favorite dinner, so maybe I'd make pasta with five cheeses and an apple and pear cobbler for dessert if that's what the honoree loves most. It makes them feel good and it says "I love you" without saying the words.

Next, I think of the season. No one wants to eat an ice-cold slice of watermelon in the winter or a steamy beef stew in August. I adore the change of seasons in East Hampton and I like to serve what's growing at the time. In the fall, when Mr. Iacono raises capons, I'll choose roast capon and serve it with carrots and potatoes from Jim Pike's farm and a tart of Macoun apples from the Halsey family's Milk Pail apple orchard. In the summer, when the fishermen are out in their boats, I'll grill lobsters and salmon and serve them with tomatoes and basil from my own garden.

I tend to build a menu starting with the main course and then work backward to the appetizers and forward to the dessert. If I decide to make loin of pork with fennel for the main course, I think about three things when I'm deciding on the side dishes: color, flavor, and texture. Pork tends to be a little bland but the fennel does have a distinct taste. However, it's also very white, so . . . maybe something creamy and yellow such as creamy rosemary polenta. Then I want something green and crunchy, so broccoli rabe with garlic will be good. I also think about what the flavors will taste like together so I don't end up with three garlicky dishes for dinner. Now for the appetizer: maybe smoked salmon with brown bread or shrimp with cocktail sauce to add some seafood to the menu. And since the dinner is a little rich, I'll choose something light for dessert such as chocolate angel food cake. It's the right food at the right time and it will all be delicious together.

Finally, I think about whether I can make it all with only one oven. The smoked salmon and shrimp are store-bought and served at room temperature, so that's no problem. The loin of pork roasts in the oven and rests at room temperature, so that's okay, too. I can make the polenta in advance and reheat it on top of the stove while I'm sautéeing the broccoli rabe. Finally, I can make the angel food cake early in the day and have it ready for dessert. Perfect! I know that I'll have a really special dinner that I can make with the confidence that it will all work perfectly together.

garlic & herb tomatoes

SERVES 6

In the summer when my favorite farmstands, Jim Pike and the Green Thumb, offer heirloom cherry tomatoes, I love to give them a quick toss in the sauté pan with lots of fresh herbs. Off season, when you can get good cherry or grape tomatoes from California and Israel, this brings out their best flavor.

3 tablespoons	good olive oil
2 teaspoons	minced garlic (2 cloves)
2 pints	cherry tomatoes or grape tomatoes
2 tablespoons	chopped fresh basil, plus more for garnish
2 tablespoons	chopped fresh flat-leaf parsley, plus more for garnish
2 teaspoons	chopped fresh thyme leaves
1 teaspoon	kosher salt
¼ teaspoon	freshly ground black pepper

Heat the olive oil in a sauté pan large enough to hold all the tomatoes in one layer. Add the garlic to the oil and cook over medium heat for 30 seconds. Add the tomatoes, basil, parsley, thyme, salt, and pepper. Reduce the heat to low and cook for 5 to 7 minutes, tossing occasionally, until the tomatoes begin to lose their firm round shape. Sprinkle with a little fresh chopped basil and parsley and serve hot or at room temperature.

orange-honey glazed carrots

SERVES 4 TO 5

As vegetables go, carrots tend to be sweet, so I decided to add honey to bring out the sweetness and ginger to balance it with spice. Freshly grated orange zest gives the dish depth. Carrots with the greens still attached are always sweeter than bagged ones.

2 pounds	carrots, peeled (3 bunches)
2 tablespoons	unsalted butter
2 tablespoons	honey
	kosher salt
1 teaspoon	minced fresh ginger
1 teaspoon	grated orange zest
½ cup	freshly squeezed orange juice
½ teaspoon	freshly ground black pepper

This dish reheats beautifully. Undercook the carrots a bit and reheat them before serving.

For a crowd, multiply the recipe and use a larger sauté pan. The carrots may take a little longer to cook.

Cut the carrots diagonally in 1-inch-thick slices. You should have about 5 cups of carrots. Place ½ cup water, the butter, honey, 2 teaspoons of salt, and the ginger in a large sauté pan and bring to a boil. Add the carrots, cover, and simmer over medium-low heat for 5 minutes. Remove the lid and continue to cook for 10 to 15 minutes, until all the water has evaporated.

Add the orange zest and orange juice to the pan, tossing with the carrots. Simmer uncovered for about 5 minutes, until the carrots are al dente (tender but still resistant when you bite) and the sauce glazes the carrots. Add the pepper and another teaspoon of salt, to taste.

broccolini & balsamic vinaigrette

SERVES 6

My dear friend and business partner Frank Newbold claims he doesn't know how to cook, but I know the truth. This broccolini (sometimes called baby broccoli) with a balsamic vinaigrette is his creation and it's delicious served hot as a side dish or cold as a summer salad.

	kosher salt
4 bunches	broccolini (1½ pounds)
¼ cup	good olive oil
1½ tablespoons	balsamic vinegar
½ teaspoon	Dijon mustard
1 teaspoon	minced garlic
½ teaspoon	freshly ground black pepper
1	lemon

Choose broccolini that's bright green, with firm, closed florets and firm stalks.

In a large pot, bring 8 cups water and 2 tablespoons salt to a boil. Remove and discard the bottom third of the broccolini stems. If some stems are very thick, cut them in half lengthwise.

Meanwhile, in a small bowl, whisk together the olive oil, balsamic vinegar, mustard, garlic, 1½ teaspoons salt, and the pepper. When the water comes to a full boil, add the broccolini, return to a boil, and cook over high heat for 2 minutes, until the stalks are *just* tender. Drain well and place in a large bowl. Pour enough dressing over the broccolini to moisten and toss well. Splash with a generous squeeze of fresh lemon juice, sprinkle with salt, and serve warm or cold.

zucchini pancakes

MAKES 10 (3-INCH) PANCAKES

My mother used to make zucchini pancakes and I always loved them. They're a good way to get vegetables into your kids—never mind being a great use for all those enormous zucchini in your garden!

2 medium	zucchini (about ¾ pound)
2 tablespoons	grated red onion
2	extra-large eggs, lightly beaten
6 to 8 tablespoons	all-purpose flour
1 teaspoon	baking powder
1 teaspoon	kosher salt
½ teaspoon	freshly ground black pepper
	unsalted butter and vegetable oil

Zucchini doesn't need to be peeled.

Preheat the oven to 300 degrees.

Grate the zucchini into a bowl using the large grating side of a box grater. Immediately stir in the onion and eggs. Stir in 6 tablespoons of the flour, the baking powder, salt, and pepper. (If the batter gets too thin from the liquid in the zucchini, add the remaining 2 tablespoons of flour.)

Heat a large (10- to 12-inch) sauté pan over medium heat and melt ½ tablespoon butter and ½ tablespoon oil together in the pan. When the butter is hot but not smoking, lower the heat to medium-low and drop heaping soup spoons of batter into the pan. Cook the pancakes about 2 minutes on each side, until browned. Place the pancakes on a sheet pan and keep warm in the oven. Wipe out the pan with a dry paper towel, add more butter and oil to the pan, and continue to fry the pancakes until all the batter is used. The pancakes can stay warm in the oven for up to 30 minutes. Serve hot.

herbed basmati rice

SERVES 3 TO 4

Years ago, I was making a side dish at Barefoot Contessa and I didn't think it had enough flavor. My wonderful chef Martine Sharp said something I've never forgotten. She told me that if every dish on your plate hits you in the head with flavor, it will give you a headache. Some tastes need to be quiet in order to balance with others that are strong. When I'm making Indonesian Ginger Chicken (The Barefoot Contessa Cookbook) or Loin of Pork with Fennel (page 104), this rice plays a perfect supporting role.

Basmati rice is grown in the foothills of the Himalayas and it's aged to develop its nutty, perfumy flavor. It's commonly used in Indian and Middle Eastern cooking.

1 cup	uncooked long-grain (white) basmati rice
¾ teaspoon	kosher salt
1 tablespoon	unsalted butter
2 tablespoons	minced fresh flat-leaf parsley
1 tablespoon	minced fresh dill
1 tablespoon	minced fresh scallions, white and green parts
	pinch of freshly ground black pepper

Combine the rice, 1¾ cups water, the salt, and butter in a small heavy-bottomed saucepan. Bring to a boil over high heat; reduce the heat to low, stir once, and simmer covered tightly for 15 minutes. (I need to pull the pot half off the burner to keep it from boiling over.) Turn off the heat and allow the rice to sit covered for 5 minutes. Add the parsley, dill, scallions, and pepper. Fluff with a fork, and serve warm.

green green
spring vegetables

SERVES 4 TO 6

There is a terrific group of restaurants in Paris owned by the Costes brothers. This is inspired by a dish I had at one of their restaurants, Café Ruc, which is directly across from the Louvre. You can blanch the vegetables early in the day, drain them, and store them in the refrigerator. It only takes a few minutes to sauté them with shallots before dinner.

¼ pound	French string beans (haricots verts), ends removed
	kosher salt
¼ pound	sugar snap peas, ends and strings removed
¼ pound	asparagus, ends removed
½ pound	broccolini, ends removed
2 tablespoons	unsalted butter
1 tablespoon	good olive oil
3 large	shallots, sliced
½ teaspoon	freshly ground black pepper

Blanch the string beans in a large pot of boiling salted water for 1 minute only. Lift the beans from the water with a slotted spoon or sieve and immerse them in a bowl of ice water. Add the snap peas to the same boiling water and cook for 1 minute, until al dente, adding them to the ice water and the beans. Cut the asparagus into 2-inch lengths diagonally and cook in the boiling water for 2 minutes, and add to the ice water. Cut the broccolini in half, boil for 1 minute, and add to the ice water. When all the vegetables in the water are cold, drain well.

When ready to serve, heat the butter and oil in a very large sauté pan or large pot. Sauté the shallots over medium heat for 5 minutes, tossing occasionally, until lightly browned. Add the drained vegetables to the shallots with ½ teaspoon salt and the pepper and toss. Cook just until the vegetables are heated through. Serve hot.

buttermilk
mashed potatoes

SERVES 5 TO 6

Whenever I'm in San Francisco, I have to go to Zuni Café. Judy Rodgers, the amazing founder, told me that her buttermilk mashed potatoes were so popular that whatever she pairs with them on the menu is the most popular dish that night. I came right home and made my version of her famous dish.

	kosher salt
3 pounds	boiling potatoes, such as Yukon Gold
½ cup	whole milk
¼ pound (1 stick)	unsalted butter
¾ to 1 cup	buttermilk, shaken
½ teaspoon	freshly ground black pepper

Choose potatoes that are firm and have no sprouts.

Don't be tempted to heat the buttermilk with the whole milk and cream; it will curdle.

In a large pot, bring 4 quarts water and 2 tablespoons salt to a boil. Meanwhile, peel the potatoes and cut them into 1½-inch cubes. Add them to the boiling water and bring the water back to a boil. Lower the heat and simmer uncovered for 10 to 15 minutes, until the potatoes fall apart easily when pierced with a fork.

Meanwhile, heat the whole milk and butter in a small saucepan, making sure it doesn't boil. Set aside until the potatoes are done.

As soon as the potatoes are tender, drain them in a colander. Place a food mill fitted with a small disk or blade over a heat-proof bowl. Pass the potatoes through the food mill, turning the handle back and forth. As soon as the potatoes are mashed, stir in the hot milk-and-butter mixture with a rubber spatula. Add enough buttermilk to make the potatoes creamy. Add 2 teaspoons of salt and the pepper, or more to taste, and serve hot. To keep the potatoes warm, place the bowl over a pan of simmering water for up to 30 minutes. You can add a little extra hot milk to keep them creamy.

stewed lentils
& tomatoes

SERVES 6 TO 8

Years ago I came across this recipe in a wonderful book called Spa Food *by Edward J. Safdie. Whenever I worked in the kitchen at Barefoot Contessa, I'd make huge pots of it. It's healthy and it's delicious.*

2 teaspoons	good olive oil
2 cups	large-diced yellow onions (2 onions)
2 cups	large-diced carrots (3 to 4 carrots)
1 tablespoon	minced garlic (3 cloves)
1 (28-ounce) can	whole plum tomatoes
1 cup	French green lentils (7 ounces)
2 cups	chicken stock, preferably homemade (page 45)
2 teaspoons	mild curry powder
2 teaspoons	chopped fresh thyme leaves
2 teaspoons	kosher salt
¼ teaspoon	freshly ground black pepper
1 tablespoon	good red wine vinegar

Garlic burns easily so you want to cook it for only a minute.

To remove thyme leaves from the stem, run your pinched fingertips down the stem from the top and the leaves will fall off.

Heat the oil in a large saucepan. Add the onions and carrots and cook over medium-low heat for 8 to 10 minutes, until the onions start to brown. Stir occasionally with a wooden spoon. Add the garlic and cook for 1 more minute.

Meanwhile, place the canned plum tomatoes, including the juice, in the bowl of a food processor fitted with a steel blade and pulse several times until the tomatoes are coarsely chopped. Rinse and pick over the lentils to make sure there are no stones in the package.

Add the tomatoes, lentils, chicken broth, curry powder, thyme, salt, and pepper to the pan. Raise the heat to bring to a boil, then lower the heat and simmer covered for about 40 minutes, until the lentils are tender. Check occasionally to be sure the liquid is still simmering. Remove from the heat and allow the lentils to sit covered for another 10 minutes. Add the vinegar, season to taste, and serve hot.

parmesan-roasted cauliflower

SERVES 6

I don't especially like cauliflower, and for years, the only way I'd eat it was smothered in cream sauce. Until, that is, I learned that roasting it at a high temperature makes it sweeter and gets rid of that chalky texture. A sprinkling of Parmesan and Gruyère at the end doesn't hurt, either.

1 large head	cauliflower
3 tablespoons	good olive oil
	kosher salt and freshly ground black pepper
1 cup	freshly grated Parmesan cheese (2 ounces)
1 cup	freshly grated Gruyère cheese (2 ounces)

Grate the Parmesan and Gruyère on the coarse side of a box grater for this dish.

Preheat the oven to 350 degrees.

Remove the outer green leaves from the cauliflower and cut the head into florets, discarding the stems. Place the florets on a sheet pan. Drizzle with the olive oil and sprinkle generously with salt and pepper. Toss well. Bake for 30 minutes, tossing once, until the cauliflower is tender and starts to brown. Sprinkle with the Parmesan and Gruyère and bake for 1 to 2 more minutes, just until the cheese melts. Season to taste and serve hot or warm.

creamy rosemary polenta

SERVES 6

Polenta can be served either firm—sautéed in a cake form—or creamy like mashed potatoes. Everyone says you can't reheat polenta, but I make this all the time and I reheat it slowly in a saucepan with some added chicken stock. It's absolutely delicious with roast chicken or roast pork. (For photograph, see page 126.)

4 cups	chicken stock, preferably homemade (page 45)
1 teaspoon	minced garlic
1 cup	yellow cornmeal
½ cup	Philadelphia whipped cream cheese
⅓ cup	freshly grated Parmesan cheese, plus extra for serving
2 tablespoons	good olive oil
1 tablespoon	chopped fresh rosemary
1 teaspoon	kosher salt
½ teaspoon	freshly ground black pepper

I use Quaker yellow cornmeal; if you have a choice, choose "medium" rather than coarse or fine.

To reheat polenta, place the cold mixture in a pot with extra chicken stock and reheat slowly over low heat, stirring until smooth.

Heat the chicken stock in a medium saucepan. Add the garlic and cook over medium-high heat until the stock comes to a boil. Reduce the heat to medium-low and very slowly add the cornmeal, whisking constantly with a wire whisk to make sure there are no lumps. Switch to a wooden spoon and simmer over very low heat, stirring almost constantly, for 7 to 10 minutes, until thick. Be sure to scrape the bottom of the pan thoroughly while you're stirring. Remove the polenta from the heat and stir in the cream cheese, Parmesan, olive oil, rosemary, salt, and pepper. Stir until smooth and serve hot sprinkled with extra Parmesan cheese.

broccoli rabe with garlic

SERVES 4 TO 5

Broccoli rabe is an Italian vegetable that looks a little like American broccoli but is more bitter. It's actually a member of the cabbage family and it's in season throughout the fall and winter. I love to sauté it in olive oil with lots of garlic.

2 bunches	broccoli rabe
3 tablespoons	good olive oil
6 large	garlic cloves, sliced
½ teaspoon	crushed red pepper flakes
2 teaspoons	kosher salt
½ teaspoon	freshly ground black pepper

Cut off and discard the tough ends of the broccoli rabe and cut the rest of it into 2-inch pieces. Place the broccoli in a colander and rinse. Drain well.

Heat the olive oil in a large pot. Add the garlic and cook over low heat, stirring occasionally, for 4 to 6 minutes, until golden brown. Remove the garlic with a slotted spoon, and set aside.

Add the broccoli to the hot oil. Add the red pepper flakes, salt, and pepper and cook covered over medium to low heat for 5 to 10 minutes, turning occasionally with tongs, until the stalks are tender but still al dente. Add the reserved garlic, check the seasonings, and serve hot.

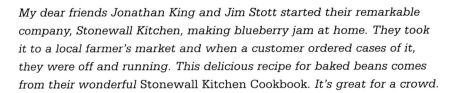

maple baked beans

SERVES 8

My dear friends Jonathan King and Jim Stott started their remarkable company, Stonewall Kitchen, making blueberry jam at home. They took it to a local farmer's market and when a customer ordered cases of it, they were off and running. This delicious recipe for baked beans comes from their wonderful Stonewall Kitchen Cookbook. *It's great for a crowd.*

1 pound	dry red kidney beans
1 large	yellow onion, cut in eighths
1	bay leaf
6	whole black peppercorns
¾ cup	medium amber pure maple syrup
½ cup	light brown sugar, lightly packed
½ cup	ketchup
1 tablespoon	Chinese chili paste
1 tablespoon	grated fresh ginger
1 teaspoon	kosher salt
5 ounces	thick-cut smoked bacon, cubed

Place the beans in a large bowl and cover with cold water by 1 inch and cover with plastic wrap. Refrigerate overnight. Drain and rinse the beans and then drain again.

Place the beans in a large pot with 2 quarts water, the onion, bay leaf, and peppercorns. Bring to a boil, then lower the heat and simmer for about 50 minutes, or until tender. A good test is to scoop up several beans in a spoon and blow on them: if the skins start to peel off, they're done. Drain the beans, reserving the cooking liquid.

Preheat the oven to 225 degrees.

In a small saucepan, whisk together the maple syrup, brown sugar, ketchup, chili paste, ginger, salt, and 1½ cups of the cooking liquid, still reserving the remaining liquid. Bring to a simmer and cook over medium heat for 6 minutes.

Transfer the beans to a medium Dutch oven or a bean pot. Push half the bacon into the beans and place the rest on the top. Pour the maple syrup sauce over the beans. Place the lid on top and bake for 6 to 8 hours. Check occasionally; if the beans are too dry, add ½ cup more of the cooking liquid. If you like, you can remove the lid for the last 30 minutes to thicken the sauce. Discard the bay leaf. Serve hot.

A Le Creuset Dutch oven is perfect for baking this dish.

mustard-roasted potatoes

SERVES 6

Roasting potatoes at high heat makes them crisp on the outside and tender inside. If you want to prep the potatoes early, store them covered in water to keep them from turning brown. When you're ready to roast them, drain the water and add lots of mustard and seasonings.

2½ pounds	small red potatoes
2	yellow onions
3 tablespoons	good olive oil
2 tablespoons	whole-grain mustard
	kosher salt
1 teaspoon	freshly ground black pepper
¼ cup	chopped fresh flat-leaf parsley

Preheat the oven to 425 degrees.

Cut the potatoes in halves or quarters, depending on their size, and place them on a sheet pan. Remove the ends of the onions, peel them, and cut them in half. Slice them crosswise in ¼-inch-thick slices to make half-rounds. Toss the onions and potatoes together on the sheet pan. Add the olive oil, mustard, 2 teaspoons salt, and the pepper and toss them together. Bake for 50 minutes to 1 hour, until the potatoes are lightly browned on the outside and tender on the inside. Toss the potatoes from time to time with a metal spatula so they brown evenly.

Serve hot sprinkled with the chopped parsley and a little extra salt.

jalapeño cheddar cornbread

MAKES 12 LARGE PIECES

Most cornbread is dry and tasteless, but this one stays moist from the Cheddar and milk and has a nice kick from the scallions and jalapeño peppers. We used to sell big chunks of it at Barefoot Contessa; they're particularly great in the summer with barbecued chicken and ribs.

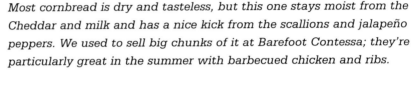

3 cups	all-purpose flour
1 cup	yellow cornmeal
¼ cup	sugar
2 tablespoons	baking powder
2 teaspoons	kosher salt
2 cups	milk
3	extra-large eggs, lightly beaten
½ pound (2 sticks)	unsalted butter, melted, plus extra to grease the pan
8 ounces	aged extra-sharp Cheddar, grated, divided
⅓ cup	chopped scallions, white and green parts, plus extra for garnish (3 scallions)
3 tablespoons	seeded and minced fresh jalapeño peppers (2 to 3 peppers)

Grate the Cheddar on a box grater. Yellow Cheddar will look better but extra-sharp white Cheddar will have more flavor.

Change your baking powder every few months to make sure it's active.

When measuring pans, every manufacturer measures differently. I measure the inside dimensions.

Combine the flour, cornmeal, sugar, baking powder, and salt in a large bowl. In a separate bowl, combine the milk, eggs, and butter. With a wooden spoon, stir the wet ingredients into the dry until most of the lumps are dissolved. Don't overmix! Mix in 2 cups of the grated Cheddar, the scallions, and jalapeños, and allow the mixture to sit at room temperature for 20 minutes.

Meanwhile, preheat the oven to 350 degrees. Grease a 9 × 13 × 2-inch baking pan.

Pour the batter into the prepared pan, smooth the top, and sprinkle with the remaining grated Cheddar and extra chopped scallions. Bake for 30 to 35 minutes, or until a toothpick comes out clean. Cool and cut into large squares. Serve warm or at room temperature.

herb-roasted onions

SERVES 6

Serving onions as a vegetable is a little unusual. Fried onion rings or creamed onions maybe, but roasted onions? You bet! They're surprisingly delicious and a very inexpensive side dish.

4	red onions
3	yellow onions
¼ cup	freshly squeezed lemon juice (2 lemons)
2 teaspoons	Dijon mustard
2 teaspoons	minced garlic (2 cloves)
1 tablespoon	minced fresh thyme leaves
1½ teaspoons	kosher salt
½ teaspoon	freshly ground black pepper
½ cup	good olive oil
1 tablespoon	minced fresh flat-leaf parsley

Preheat the oven to 400 degrees.

Remove the stem end of each onion and carefully slice off the brown part of the root end, leaving the root intact. Peel the onions. Stand each onion root end up on a cutting board and cut the onions in wedges through the root. Place the wedges in a large bowl.

Combine the lemon juice, mustard, garlic, thyme, salt, and pepper in a small bowl. Slowly whisk in the olive oil. Pour the dressing over the onions and toss well.

With a slotted spoon, transfer the onions to a sheet pan, reserving the vinaigrette that remains in the bowl. Bake the onions for 30 to 45 minutes, until tender and browned. Toss the onions once during cooking. Remove from the oven and drizzle with the reserved dressing. Sprinkle with parsley, season to taste, and serve warm or at room temperature.

dessert

frozen berries with hot white chocolate

beatty's chocolate cake

lemon yogurt cake

peanut butter & jelly bars

mixed berry pavlova

coconut cake

pumpkin mousse parfait

chocolate sorbet

black & white angel food cake

chocolate cupcakes & peanut butter icing

panna cotta with balsamic strawberries

ultimate ginger cookie

fruitcake cookies

peach & blueberry crumbles

pear, apple & cranberry crisp

summer fruit crostata

caramel pecan sundaes

developing a recipe

I've always liked science. In high school, I was an okay student, but when it came time for the annual science fair, I came alive. The nerdy boys in my class would spend the entire year studying something really important for their projects, like how to cure cancer. I, on the other hand, would throw together some crazy experiment a month before the science fair and I'd win all the prizes. It made the boys nuts. Looking back, I realize that while all the guys were going to the library and studying what had already been done, I was more interested in experimenting to develop something new. I'd form a hypothesis, set something up to test my theory, and then take notes on the results. Frankly, I thought it was more interesting than going to the library, although I'm not so sure my mother was thrilled with feeding the twenty-five white mice I used for my project one year!

For me, cooking isn't all that different from those high school science projects except that, instead of hydrochloric acid, you end up with chocolate cupcakes. When I'm working on a recipe, I use the same process I followed to set up a science experiment. First, I form a hypothesis in my head of what I want something to look and taste like. I might be working on chocolate angel food cake: Can a cake be both flavorful and light at the same time? Next, I'll read everything I can about angel food cakes: What temperature should the ingredients be? How does the leavening

interact with the egg whites? Will humidity affect the outcome? When I have a clear vision in mind, a theory about how to achieve it, and lots of good information to back up my theory, I'll put it to the test—I'll roll up my sleeves and bake angel food cake after angel food cake. Each time, I change one variable—maybe increase the salt or decrease the baking powder—and I learn what works and what doesn't. And, just like with all good science experiments, I keep my eye out for surprises because sometimes it's the accidents that yield the most interesting results. I can spend an entire week experimenting with one recipe.

Even when I'm not developing recipes I love to take a single idea and play with it. The idea can be something that I've never tried before, like a Pavlova, which is a disk of baked meringue piled high with whipped cream and fresh fruit. Or the idea can be a recipe that I just want to evolve—like turning my old-fashioned apple crisp into a pear, apple, and cranberry crisp. But just as with my old science projects, there's a great pleasure in developing my own ideas rather than always relying on what other people have written. I hope you start with the recipes in this book and experiment a little to develop your own recipes that will become new family favorites. How cool would that be?

frozen berries with hot white chocolate

SERVES 6

My British television producers introduced me to this delicious concoction; it's hot white chocolate poured over frozen berries and it's served at two of London's most popular restaurants, The Ivy and J. Sheekey's. The combination of cold and hot is amazing. You can also use frozen berries; the individually flash-frozen kind are available in the freezer section of many grocery stores.

2 half-pints	fresh raspberries
2 half-pints	fresh blueberries
1 pint	fresh strawberries, hulled and sliced thick
1 cup	heavy cream
10 ounces	good white chocolate (not chips), chopped
½ teaspoon	pure vanilla extract

I use Callebaut or Lindt white chocolate.

The chocolate can be melted early and then reheated over simmering water to 110 degrees. Don't overheat or the chocolate will separate and burn.

Early in the day, spread the berries on a sheet pan in a single layer and place them in the freezer. (This prevents them from sticking together.) Once they're frozen, store them in a freezer bag.

In a heat-proof bowl set over a pan of simmering water, heat the cream, white chocolate, and vanilla just until the chocolate melts. Don't let the bowl touch the water. Heat the mixture until it's warm to the touch, about 110 degrees.

Place the frozen berries in one layer on 6 dessert plates and allow them to sit at room temperature for 10 to 15 minutes to defrost slightly. Pour the hot white chocolate evenly over the frozen berries and serve immediately.

beatty's chocolate cake

SERVES 8

Michael Grimm from Bridgehampton Florist made this wonderful chocolate cake for me. His grandfather used to have a milk route in Pennsylvania Dutch country and his grandmother baked this chocolate cake for him to deliver to customers with their milk. It's so chocolatey and the secret is a cup of hot coffee in the batter.

	butter for greasing the pans
1¾ cups	all-purpose flour, plus more for the pans
2 cups	sugar
¾ cup	good cocoa powder
2 teaspoons	baking soda
1 teaspoon	baking powder
1 teaspoon	kosher salt
1 cup	buttermilk, shaken
½ cup	vegetable oil
2	extra-large eggs, at room temperature
1 teaspoon	pure vanilla extract
1 cup	freshly brewed hot coffee
	Chocolate Frosting (page 167)

The pans I use are deep, with 2-inch sides. If you don't have deep pans, use 9-inch pans to ensure the batter does not overflow. The cake won't be as high but it will be just as delicious

Preheat the oven to 350 degrees. Butter two 8 × 2-inch round cake pans. Line with parchment paper, then butter and flour the pans.

Sift the flour, sugar, cocoa, baking soda, baking powder, and salt into the bowl of an electric mixer fitted with a paddle attachment and mix on low speed until combined. In another bowl, combine the buttermilk, oil, eggs, and vanilla. With the mixer on low speed, slowly add the wet ingredients to the dry. With the mixer still on low, add the coffee and stir just to combine, scraping the bottom of the bowl with a rubber spatula. Pour the batter into the prepared pans and bake for 35 to 40 minutes, until a cake tester comes out clean. Cool in the pans for 30 minutes, then turn them out onto a cooling rack and cool completely.

Place one layer, flat side up, on a flat plate or cake pedestal. With a knife or offset spatula, spread the top with frosting. Place the second layer on top, rounded side up, and spread the frosting evenly on the top and sides of the cake.

chocolate frosting

6 ounces	good semisweet chocolate such as Callebaut
½ pound (2 sticks)	unsalted butter, at room temperature
1	extra-large egg yolk, at room temperature
1 teaspoon	pure vanilla extract
1¼ cups	sifted confectioners' sugar
1 tablespoon	instant coffee powder

Chop the chocolate and place it in a heat-proof bowl set over a pan of simmering water. Stir until just melted and set aside until cooled to room temperature.

In the bowl of an electric mixer fitted with a paddle attachment, beat the butter on medium-high speed until light yellow and fluffy, about 3 minutes. Add the egg yolk and vanilla and continue beating for 3 minutes. Turn the mixer to low, gradually add the confectioners' sugar, then beat at medium speed, scraping down the bowl as necessary, until smooth and creamy. Dissolve the coffee powder in 2 teaspoons of the hottest tap water. On low speed, add the chocolate and coffee to the butter mixture and mix until blended. Don't whip! Spread immediately on the cooled cake.

You can use any good semisweet chocolate, but don't use chocolate chips because they contain stabilizers.

lemon yogurt cake

MAKES 1 LOAF

Despite my reputation for starting all my recipes with a pound of butter, I really do look for ways to make desserts lighter. When I came across a delicious yogurt cake by cookbook author Dorie Greenspan, I decided to see if I could update my favorite lemon cake with her method of using yogurt and vegetable oil instead of butter. Not only is it good for you, but you don't even need an electric mixer to make it!

1½ cups	all-purpose flour
2 teaspoons	baking powder
½ teaspoon	kosher salt
1 cup	plain whole-milk yogurt
1⅓ cups	sugar, divided
3	extra-large eggs
2 teaspoons	grated lemon zest (2 lemons)
½ teaspoon	pure vanilla extract
½ cup	vegetable oil
⅓ cup	freshly squeezed lemon juice

For the glaze

1 cup	confectioners' sugar
2 tablespoons	freshly squeezed lemon juice

Preheat the oven to 350 degrees. Grease an 8½ × 4¼ × 2½-inch loaf pan. Line the bottom with parchment paper. Grease and flour the pan.

Sift together the flour, baking powder, and salt into one bowl. In another bowl, whisk together the yogurt, 1 cup sugar, the eggs, lemon zest, and vanilla. Slowly whisk the dry ingredients into the wet ingredients. With a rubber spatula, fold the vegetable oil into the batter, making sure it's all incorporated. Pour the batter into the prepared pan and bake for about 50 minutes, or until a cake tester placed in the center of the loaf comes out clean.

Meanwhile, cook the ⅓ cup lemon juice and remaining ⅓ cup sugar in a small pan until the sugar dissolves and the mixture is clear. Set aside.

When the cake is done, allow it to cool in the pan for 10 minutes. Carefully place on a baking rack over a sheet pan. While the cake is still warm, pour the lemon-sugar mixture over the cake and allow it to soak in. Cool.

For the glaze, combine the confectioners' sugar and lemon juice and pour over the cake.

peanut butter & jelly bars

MAKES 24 BARS

I'd always had the idea of making a peanut butter and jelly bar when I came across one in Martha Stewart Living *magazine that inspired me. These are really rich and delicious and will appeal to the "inner child" in everyone.*

½ pound (2 sticks)	unsalted butter, at room temperature, plus more for greasing the pan
1½ cups	sugar
1 teaspoon	pure vanilla extract
2	extra-large eggs, at room temperature
2 cups	creamy peanut butter, such as Skippy (18 ounces)
3 cups	all-purpose flour, plus more for dusting the pan
1 teaspoon	baking powder
1½ teaspoons	kosher salt
1½ cups	raspberry jam or other jam (18 ounces)
⅔ cups	salted peanuts, coarsely chopped

Preheat the oven to 350 degrees. Grease and flour a 9 × 13 × 2-inch baking pan.

In the bowl of an electric mixer fitted with a paddle attachment, cream the butter and sugar on medium speed until light yellow, about 2 minutes. With the mixer on low speed, add the vanilla, eggs, and peanut butter and mix until well combined.

In a small bowl, sift together the flour, baking powder, and salt. With the mixer on low speed, slowly add the flour mixture to the peanut butter mixture. Mix just until combined.

Spread two thirds of the dough in the prepared pan, using a knife to spread it evenly. Spread the jam evenly over the dough. Drop small globs of the remaining dough evenly over the jam.

Don't worry if all the jam isn't covered; the dough will spread when it bakes. Sprinkle with the chopped peanuts and bake for 45 minutes, until golden brown. Cool and cut into small squares.

mixed berry pavlova

SERVES 6

I'm always looking for easy fruit desserts. Pavlova is an Australian dessert named for the famed Russian ballerina Anna Pavlova—probably because it looks like her tutu. It's a meringue disk that's slathered with whipped cream and topped with fresh fruit—often passion fruit. But who wants to hunt for passion fruit? Instead, I pile it high with lots of fresh berries and my favorite raspberry sauce. Delicious.

4	extra-large egg whites, at room temperature
	pinch of kosher salt
1 cup	sugar
2 teaspoons	cornstarch
1 teaspoon	white wine vinegar
½ teaspoon	pure vanilla extract
	Sweetened Whipped Cream (page 175)
½ pint	fresh strawberries, hulled and sliced
½ pint	fresh blueberries
½ pint	fresh raspberries
	Triple Raspberry Sauce (page 175)

Preheat the oven to 180 degrees. Place a sheet of parchment paper on a sheet pan. Draw a 9-inch circle on the paper, using a 9-inch plate as a guide, then turn the paper over so the circle is on the reverse side. (This way you won't get a pencil mark on the meringue.)

Place the egg whites and salt in the bowl of an electric mixer fitted with a whisk attachment. Beat the egg whites on high speed until firm, about 1 minute. With the mixer still on high, slowly add the sugar and beat until it makes firm, shiny peaks, about 2 minutes.

Remove the bowl from the mixer, sift the cornstarch onto the beaten egg whites, add the vinegar and vanilla, and fold in lightly with a rubber spatula. Pile the meringue into the middle of the circle on the parchment paper and smooth it within the circle, making a rough disk. Bake for 1½ hours. Turn off the oven, keep the door closed, and allow the meringue to cool completely in the oven, about 1 hour. It will be crisp on the outside and soft inside.

Don't be tempted to mix the berries and raspberry sauce in advance; they'll become watery.

Invert the meringue disk onto a plate and spread the top completely with sweetened whipped cream. Combine the strawberries, blueberries, and raspberries in a bowl and toss with about ½ cup of raspberry sauce, or enough to coat the berries lightly. Spoon the berries carefully into the middle of the Pavlova, leaving a border of cream and meringue. Serve immediately in large scoops with extra raspberry sauce.

sweetened whipped cream

MAKES 2 CUPS

1 cup	cold heavy cream
1 tablespoon	sugar
1 teaspoon	pure vanilla extract

Whip the cream in the bowl of an electric mixer fitted with a whisk attachment (you can also use a hand mixer). When it starts to thicken, add the sugar and vanilla and continue to beat until firm. Don't overbeat!

triple raspberry sauce

MAKES 2 CUPS

½ pint	fresh raspberries
½ cup	sugar
1 cup	seedless raspberry jam (12-ounce jar)
1 tablespoon	framboise liqueur

Place the raspberries, sugar, and ¼ cup water in a small saucepan. Bring to a boil, lower the heat, and simmer for 4 minutes. Pour the cooked raspberries, the jam, and framboise into the bowl of a food processor fitted with a steel blade and process until smooth. Chill.

coconut cake

SERVES 10 TO 12

One of the signature dishes at Barefoot Contessa was coconut cupcakes and the recipe is in my first book, The Barefoot Contessa Cookbook. *So many people e-mailed me to ask if it could be made into a cake that I made some adjustments and included it here. It seems to be everyone's favorite birthday cake.*

¾ pound (3 sticks)	unsalted butter, at room temperature, plus more for greasing the pans
2 cups	sugar
5	extra-large eggs, at room temperature
1½ teaspoons	pure vanilla extract
1½ teaspoons	pure almond extract
3 cups	all-purpose flour, plus more for dusting the pans
1 teaspoon	baking powder
½ teaspoon	baking soda
½ teaspoon	kosher salt
1 cup	milk
4 ounces	sweetened shredded coconut

For the frosting

1 pound	cream cheese, at room temperature
½ pound (2 sticks)	unsalted butter, at room temperature
¾ teaspoon	pure vanilla extract
¼ teaspoon	pure almond extract
1 pound	confectioners' sugar, sifted
6 ounces	sweetened shredded coconut

To make in advance, bake the cakes and wrap them well. Refrigerate for up to 5 days. Ice the cake before serving and serve at room temperature.

Preheat the oven to 350 degrees. Grease two 9-inch round cake pans, then line them with parchment paper. Grease them again and dust lightly with flour.

In the bowl of an electric mixer fitted with a paddle attachment, cream the butter and sugar on medium-high speed for 3 to 5 minutes, until light yellow and fluffy. Crack the eggs into a small bowl. With the mixer on medium speed, add the eggs one at a time, scraping down the bowl once during mixing. Add the vanilla and almond extracts and mix well. The mixture might look curdled; don't be concerned.

In a separate bowl, sift together the flour, baking powder, baking soda, and salt. With the mixer on low speed, alternately add the dry ingredients and the milk to the batter in three parts, beginning and ending with the dry ingredients. Mix until *just* combined. Fold in the 4 ounces of coconut with a rubber spatula.

Pour the batter evenly into the 2 pans and smooth the top with a knife. Bake in the center of the oven for 45 to 55 minutes, until the tops are browned and a cake tester comes out clean. Cool on a baking rack for 30 minutes, then turn the cakes out onto a baking rack to finish cooling.

For the frosting, in the bowl of an electric mixer fitted with a paddle attachment, combine the cream cheese, butter, vanilla, and almond extract on low speed. Add the confectioners' sugar and mix until just smooth (don't whip!).

To assemble, place one layer on a flat serving plate, top side down, and spread with frosting. Place the second layer on top, top side up, and frost the top and sides. To decorate the cake, sprinkle the top with coconut and lightly press more coconut onto the sides. Serve at room temperature.

pumpkin mousse parfait

SERVES 8 TO 10

I'm always looking for holiday desserts that aren't the usual pumpkin and pecan pies, and besides, who really likes to make pie crust? I decided to make a pumpkin mousse and layer it with whipped cream and chopped ginger cookies. It certainly wasn't the worst dessert I'd ever invented.

¼ cup	dark rum
1 packet (2 teaspoons)	unflavored gelatin powder
1 (15-ounce) can	pumpkin (not pie filling)
½ cup	granulated sugar
½ cup	light brown sugar, lightly packed
2	extra-large egg yolks
2 teaspoons	grated orange zest
½ teaspoon	ground cinnamon
¼ teaspoon	ground nutmeg
½ teaspoon	kosher salt
1½ cups	cold heavy cream
1½ teaspoons	pure vanilla extract
	Sweetened Whipped Cream (page 175)
8 to 10	chopped Ultimate Ginger Cookies (page 192 or store-bought)
	crystallized ginger, for decoration (optional)

Place the rum in a heat-proof bowl and sprinkle the gelatin over it. Set aside for 10 minutes for the gelatin to soften.

In a large bowl, whisk together the pumpkin, granulated sugar, brown sugar, egg yolks, orange zest, cinnamon, nutmeg, and salt. Set the bowl of gelatin over a pan of simmering water and cook until the gelatin is clear. Immediately whisk the hot gelatin mixture into the pumpkin mixture. In the bowl of an electric mixer fitted with a whisk attachment, whip the heavy cream and vanilla on high speed until soft peaks form. Fold the whipped cream into the pumpkin mixture.

To assemble, spoon some of the pumpkin mixture into parfait glasses, add a layer of whipped cream, then some chopped cookies. Repeat, ending with a third layer of pumpkin. Cover with plastic wrap and refrigerate for 4 hours or overnight. To serve, decorate with whipped cream and slivered crystallized ginger.

chocolate sorbet

MAKES ABOUT 2 QUARTS; SERVES 6

My test of whether something really tastes like chocolate is if I can taste it with my eyes closed. Usually we expect something to taste like chocolate because it looks like chocolate, but too often I'm disappointed. For me, two flavors really bring out the "chocolateness" of a recipe: coffee and cinnamon. I used both here.

2 cups	sugar
1 cup	very good cocoa powder, such as Pernigotti
½ teaspoon	pure vanilla extract
¼ teaspoon	ground cinnamon
¼ teaspoon	kosher salt
½ cup	brewed espresso (2 shots)
1 tablespoon	coffee liqueur, such as Tia Maria

In a large saucepan, mix the sugar, cocoa powder, vanilla, cinnamon, and salt. Stir in 4 cups water and the espresso. Cook over low heat until the ingredients are dissolved. Off the heat, stir in the coffee liqueur. Transfer to plastic containers and refrigerate until very cold.

Freeze the mixture in 2 batches in an ice cream freezer according to the manufacturer's directions. The sorbet will still be soft; place it in plastic containers and freeze for an hour or overnight, until firm enough to scoop.

Since cocoa powder is the key ingredient here, you'll want to use a good one. Williams-Sonoma sells Pernigotti cocoa powder from Italy.

I use a double shot of espresso from Starbucks but you can also substitute 2 teaspoons of instant espresso powder dissolved in ½ cup of boiling water for the brewed espresso.

black & white angel food cake

SERVES 8

Angel food cake usually tastes like cotton, so I love to infuse it with lots of flavor. Don't make this on a rainy day! It will be dense and sticky instead of light and airy. If you can't find superfine sugar, put granulated sugar into the food processor fitted with a steel blade and process it for 30 seconds.

2 cups	sifted superfine sugar (about 1 pound)
1⅓ cups	sifted cake flour (not self-rising)
1½ cups	egg whites at room temperature (10 to 12 eggs)
¾ teaspoon	kosher salt
1½ teaspoons	cream of tartar
1 teaspoon	pure vanilla extract
½ cup	coarsely grated semisweet chocolate (2 ounces)

For the glaze

½ pound	semisweet chocolate chips
¾ cup plus 1 tablespoon	heavy cream

Preheat the oven to 350 degrees.

Combine ½ cup of the sugar with the flour and sift them together 4 times. Set aside.

Place the egg whites, salt, and cream of tartar in the bowl of an electric mixer fitted with a whisk attachment and beat on high speed until the eggs form medium-firm peaks, about 1 minute. With the mixer on medium speed, add the remaining 1½ cups sugar by sprinkling it over the beaten egg whites. Beat on high speed for a few minutes, until thick and shiny. Add the vanilla and continue to whisk until very thick, about 1 more minute. Scrape the beaten egg whites into a large bowl. Sift one-fourth of the flour mixture over the egg whites and fold it very carefully into the batter with a rubber spatula. Continue adding the flour by fourths, sifting and folding until it's all incorporated. Fold in the grated chocolate.

Pour the batter into an ungreased 10-inch tube pan, smooth the top, and bake it for 35 to 45 minutes, until it springs back to the touch. Remove the cake from the oven and invert the pan on a cooling rack. When cool, run a thin, flexible knife around the cake to remove it from the pan.

For the chocolate glaze, place the chocolate chips and the heavy cream in a heat-proof bowl set over a pan of simmering water and stir until the chocolate melts. Pour the chocolate over the top of the cooled cake to cover the top completely and allow it to drizzle down the sides. If you have chocolate glaze left over, you can serve it on the side with the cake.

chocolate cupcakes & peanut butter icing

MAKES 14 TO 15 CUPCAKES

Kathleen King owns Tate's Bake Shop in Southampton, New York, and she's been baking her famous chocolate chip cookies since she was eleven years old. She bakes all kinds of delicious desserts, too, but her peanut butter icing sends me right to the moon. Spread it on Barefoot Contessa chocolate cupcakes and you're pushing all the right buttons.

12 tablespoons (1½ sticks)	unsalted butter, at room temperature
⅔ cup	granulated sugar
⅔ cup	light brown sugar, packed
2	extra-large eggs, at room temperature
2 teaspoons	pure vanilla extract
1 cup	buttermilk, shaken, at room temperature
½ cup	sour cream, at room temperature
2 tablespoons	brewed coffee
1¾ cups	all-purpose flour
1 cup	good cocoa powder
1½ teaspoons	baking soda
½ teaspoon	kosher salt
	Kathleen's Peanut Butter Icing (page 188)
	chopped salted peanuts, to decorate (optional)

Preheat the oven to 350 degrees. Line cupcake pans with paper liners.

In the bowl of an electric mixer fitted with a paddle attachment, cream the butter and two sugars on high speed until light and fluffy, approximately 5 minutes. Lower the speed to medium, add the eggs one at a time, then add the vanilla and mix well. In a separate bowl, whisk together the buttermilk, sour cream, and coffee. In another bowl, sift together the flour, cocoa, baking soda, and salt. On low speed, add the buttermilk mixture and the flour mixture alternately in thirds to the mixer bowl, beginning with the buttermilk mixture and ending with the flour mixture. Mix only until blended. Fold the batter with a rubber spatula to be sure it's completely blended.

Divide the batter among the cupcake pans (one rounded standard ice cream scoop per cup is the right amount). Bake in the middle of the oven for 20 to 25 minutes, until a toothpick comes out clean. Cool for 10 minutes, remove from the pans, and allow to cool completely before frosting.

Frost each cupcake with peanut butter icing and sprinkle with chopped peanuts, if desired.

kathleen's peanut butter icing

I use Skippy creamy peanut butter.

1 cup	confectioners' sugar
1 cup	creamy peanut butter
5 tablespoons	unsalted butter, at room temperature
¾ teaspoon	pure vanilla extract
¼ teaspoon	kosher salt
⅓ cup	heavy cream

Place the confectioners' sugar, peanut butter, butter, vanilla, and salt in the bowl of an electric mixer fitted with a paddle attachment. Mix on medium-low speed until creamy, scraping down the bowl with a rubber spatula as you work. Add the cream and beat on high speed until the mixture is light and smooth.

panna cotta with balsamic strawberries

SERVES 8

Mario Batali's food always knocks me out. His New York restaurant Babbo is one of my favorites—both elegant and earthy at the same time. Somewhere I came across his recipe for panna cotta with strawberries; it gets its wonderful flavor from vanilla beans and yogurt, and it inspired this recipe. It's surprising how the sweetness of the strawberries balances the acidity of the balsamic vinegar.

I use Stonybrook yogurt.

Store the used vanilla pods in a jar of sugar to make vanilla sugar.

1 packet (2 teaspoons)	unflavored gelatin powder
3 cups	heavy cream
2 cups	plain whole-milk yogurt
1½ teaspoons	pure vanilla extract
1	vanilla bean
¾ cup	sugar
4 pints (8 cups)	sliced fresh strawberries
5 tablespoons	balsamic vinegar
2 tablespoons	sugar
½ teaspoon	freshly ground black pepper
	freshly grated lemon zest, for serving

In a small bowl, sprinkle the gelatin on 3 tablespoons of cold water. Stir and set aside for 10 minutes to allow the gelatin to dissolve.

Meanwhile, in a medium bowl, whisk together 1½ cups of the cream, the yogurt, and vanilla extract. Split the vanilla bean and use the tip of a knife to scrape the seeds into the cream. Heat the remaining 1½ cups of cream and the sugar in a small saucepan and bring to a simmer over medium heat. Off the heat, add the softened gelatin to the hot cream and stir to dissolve.

Pour the hot cream–gelatin mixture into the cold cream–yogurt mixture and stir to combine. Pour into 8 (6- to 8-ounce) ramekins or custard cups and refrigerate uncovered until cold. When the panna cottas are thoroughly chilled, cover with plastic wrap and refrigerate overnight.

Thirty minutes to an hour before serving, combine the strawberries, balsamic vinegar, sugar, and pepper. Set aside at room temperature.

To serve, run a small knife around each dessert and dip the bottom of each ramekin quickly in a bowl of hot tap water. Invert each ramekin onto a dessert plate and surround the panna cotta with strawberries. Dust lightly with freshly grated lemon zest and serve.

ultimate ginger cookie

MAKES 16 COOKIES

I feel as though I've been on a lifelong quest for the perfect ginger cookie but I'm often disappointed. I finally decided to tackle them and came up with this cookie that's crisp outside, moist inside, and filled with crystallized ginger. I like these best the day they're baked, so I'll refrigerate the dough in balls and bake them whatever I need them.

You want the dry crystallized ginger, not the wet one.

2¼ cups	all-purpose flour
1 teaspoon	baking soda
2 teaspoons	ground cinnamon
1½ teaspoons	ground cloves
½ teaspoon	ground nutmeg
½ teaspoon	ground ginger
¼ teaspoon	kosher salt
1 cup	dark brown sugar, lightly packed
¼ cup	vegetable oil
⅓ cup	unsulfured molasses
1	extra-large egg, at room temperature
1¼ cups	chopped crystallized ginger (6 ounces)
	granulated sugar, for rolling the cookies

If you measure the oil before the molasses, the molasses won't stick to the cup measure

Preheat the oven to 350 degrees. Line 2 sheet pans with parchment paper.

In a large bowl, sift together the flour, baking soda, cinnamon, cloves, nutmeg, ginger, and salt and then combine the mixture with your hands. In the bowl of an electric mixer fitted with a paddle attachment, beat the brown sugar, oil, and molasses on medium speed for 5 minutes. Turn the mixer to low speed, add the egg, and beat for 1 minute. Scrape the bowl with a rubber spatula and beat for 1 more minute. With the mixer still on low, slowly add the dry ingredients to the bowl and mix on medium speed for 2 minutes. Add the crystallized ginger and mix until combined.

Scoop the dough with 2 spoons or a small ice cream scoop. With your hands, roll each cookie into a 1¾-inch ball and then flatten them lightly with your fingers. Press both sides of each cookie in granulated sugar and place them on the sheet pans. Bake for exactly 13 minutes. The cookies will be crackled on the top and soft inside. Let the cookies cool on the sheets for a minute or two, then transfer to wire racks to cool completely.

fruitcake cookies

MAKES 5 DOZEN SMALL COOKIES

Many years ago Lee Bailey, the wonderful cookbook author, gave me this recipe and asked us to make 600 pounds of cookies for him to sell at his store in Saks Fifth Avenue during Christmas. Nobody really likes fruit-cake, but they love these cookies—they're so delicious!

½ pound	dried figs
¼ pound	raisins
¼ pound	candied cherries, coarsely chopped
1 tablespoon	honey
2 tablespoons	dry sherry
1 tablespoon	freshly squeezed lemon juice
6 ounces	chopped walnuts
	kosher salt
½ pound (2 sticks)	unsalted butter, at room temperature
½ teaspoon	ground cloves
½ cup	superfine sugar
⅓ cup	light brown sugar, firmly packed
1	extra-large egg
2⅔ cups	all-purpose flour

Snip off the hard stems of the figs with scissors or a small knife and coarsely chop the figs. In a medium bowl, combine the figs, raisins, cherries, honey, sherry, lemon juice, walnuts, and a pinch of salt. Cover with plastic wrap and allow to sit overnight at room temperature.

In the bowl of an electric mixer fitted with a paddle attachment, cream the butter, cloves, superfine sugar, and brown sugar on medium speed until smooth, about 3 minutes. With the mixer on low speed, add the egg and mix until incorporated. With the mixer still on low, slowly add the flour and ¼ teaspoon salt and mix just until combined. Don't overmix! Add the fruits and nuts, including any liquid in the bowl. Divide the dough in half and place each half on the long edge of a 12 × 18-inch piece of parchment or wax paper. Roll each half into a log, 1½ to 1¾ inches thick, making an 18-inch-long roll. Refrigerate the dough for several hours, or until firm.

Preheat the oven to 350 degrees.

With a small, sharp knife, cut the logs into ½-inch-thick slices. Place the slices ½ inch apart on ungreased sheet pans and bake for 15 to 20 minutes, until lightly golden.

peach & blueberry crumbles

SERVES 5 TO 6

I have to admit, I'm really partial to fruit desserts. Cake is fine for an occasion, but give me warm, juicy fruit topped with a crisp flavorful crumble and I'm a happy camper. A dollop of good vanilla ice cream on top doesn't hurt, either. Of course, you can make one big crumble, but individual ones are a little more special.

For the fruit

2 pounds	firm, ripe peaches (6 to 8 peaches)
2 teaspoons	grated lemon zest
2 tablespoons	freshly squeezed lemon juice
½ cup	granulated sugar
¼ cup	all-purpose flour
1 cup	fresh blueberries (½ pint)

For the crumble

1 cup	all-purpose flour
⅓ cup	granulated sugar
¼ cup	light brown sugar, lightly packed
½ teaspoon	kosher salt
¼ teaspoon	ground cinnamon
¼ pound (1 stick)	cold unsalted butter, diced

Preheat the oven to 350 degrees.

Immerse the peaches in boiling water for 30 seconds to 1 minute, until their skins peel off easily. Place them immediately in cold water. Peel the peaches, slice them into thick wedges, and place them in a large bowl. Add the lemon zest, lemon juice, granulated sugar, and flour. Toss well. Gently mix in the blueberries. Allow the mixture to sit for 5 minutes. Spoon the mixture into ramekins or custard cups.

For the topping, combine the flour, granulated sugar, brown sugar, salt, cinnamon, and the butter in the bowl of an electric mixer fitted with a paddle attachment. Mix on low speed until the butter is the size of peas. Rub the mixture with your fingertips until it's in big crumbles, then sprinkle evenly over the fruit. Place the ramekins on a sheet pan lined with parchment paper and bake for 40 to 45 minutes, until the tops are browned and crisp and the juices are bubbly. Serve warm or at room temperature.

If you want to make these early, store the unbaked crumbles in the refrigerator and bake before dinner.

pear, apple & cranberry crisp

SERVES 8

My friend Elsa Walsh and her daughter Diana Woodward make this variation on my apple crisp and it's delicious! Choose ripe pears that have a full pear aroma. Bosc pears start off green and then turn brown when they're ripe. If you can't find Macoun apples, try any firm red apple.

2 pounds	ripe Bosc pears (4 pears)
2 pounds	firm Macoun apples (6 apples)
¾ cup	dried cranberries
1 teaspoon	grated orange zest
1 teaspoon	grated lemon zest
2 tablespoons	freshly squeezed orange juice
2 tablespoons	freshly squeezed lemon juice
½ cup	granulated sugar
¼ cup	all-purpose flour
1 teaspoon	ground cinnamon
½ teaspoon	ground nutmeg

For the topping

1½ cups	all-purpose flour
¾ cup	granulated sugar
¾ cup	light brown sugar, lightly packed
½ teaspoon	kosher salt
1 cup	old-fashioned oatmeal
½ pound (2 sticks)	cold unsalted butter, diced

Preheat the oven to 350 degrees.

Peel and core the pears and apples and cut them into large chunks. Place the fruit in a large bowl and toss with the cranberries, zests, juices, granulated sugar, flour, cinnamon, and nutmeg. Pour into a 9 × 12 × 2-inch baking dish.

For the topping, combine the flour, sugars, salt, oatmeal, and cold butter in the bowl of an electric mixer fitted with a paddle attachment. Mix on low speed for 1 to 2 minutes, or until the mixture is in large crumbles. Sprinkle evenly over the fruit, covering the fruit completely.

Place the baking dish on a parchment-lined sheet pan and bake for 50 minutes to 1 hour, until the top is brown and the fruit is bubbly. Serve warm.

summer fruit crostata

SERVES 6

My friends George Germon and Johanne Killeen wrote one of my favorite cookbooks called Cucina Simpatica. *They make a wonderfully easy and delicious apple crostata, so I decided to try my own variation with summer fruit. It's juicy and makes a sweet and a perfect light summer dessert.*

For the pastry (makes 2 crostatas)

2 cups	all-purpose flour
¼ cup	granulated or superfine sugar
½ teaspoon	kosher salt
½ pound (2 sticks)	cold unsalted butter, diced
6 tablespoons (3 ounces)	ice water

For the filling (makes 1 crostata)

1 pound	firm, ripe peaches, peeled
½ pound	firm, ripe black plums, unpeeled
½ pint	fresh blueberries
1 tablespoon plus ¼ cup	all-purpose flour
1 tablespoon plus ¼ cup	granulated sugar
¼ teaspoon	grated orange zest
2 tablespoons	freshly squeezed orange juice
¼ teaspoon	kosher salt
4 tablespoons (½ stick)	cold unsalted butter, diced

For the pastry, place the flour, sugar, and salt in the bowl of a food processor fitted with a steel blade. Pulse a few times to combine. Add the butter and toss quickly (and carefully!) with your fingers to coat each cube of butter with the flour. Pulse 12 to 15 times, or until the butter is the size of peas. With the motor running, add the ice water all at once through the feed tube. Keep hitting the pulse button to combine, but stop the machine just before the dough comes together. Turn the dough out onto a well-floured board, roll it into a ball, cut in half, and form into 2 flat disks. Wrap the disks in plastic and refrigerate for at least an hour. If you only need one dough, freeze the second disk.

Preheat the oven to 450 degrees. Line a sheet pan with parchment paper.

Roll the pastry into an 11-inch circle on a lightly floured surface. Transfer it to the sheet pan.

For the filling, cut the peaches and plums in wedges and place them in a bowl with the blueberries. Toss them with 1 tablespoon of the flour, 1 tablespoon of the sugar, the orange zest, and the orange juice. Place the mixed fruit on the dough circle, leaving a 1½-inch border.

Combine the ¼ cup flour, the ¼ cup sugar, and the salt in the bowl of a food processor fitted with a steel blade. Add the butter and pulse until the mixture is crumbly. Pour into a bowl and rub it with your fingers until it starts to hold together. Sprinkle evenly over the fruit. Gently fold the border of the pastry over the fruit, pleating it to make an edge.

Bake the crostata for 20 to 25 minutes, until the crust is golden and the fruit is tender. Let the crostata cool for 5 minutes, then use 2 large spatulas to transfer it to a wire rack. Serve warm or at room temperature.

YELLOW PEACHES
FIRM
BAG 5 lbs 11 95

READY 2 lb. 6 65
EAT 95
        4 lb 12

LOCAL

THE
MILK
PAIL
FARM & ORCHARD
COUNTRY STORE
U-PICK
AMY'S FLOWERS
PEACHES
APPLES

5 pounds net weight
Keep Refrigerated

caramel pecan sundaes

SERVES 6

Who doesn't love real caramel sauce? It's so easy to make and it's sooo good. I like it best over good vanilla and butter pecan ice creams topped with toasted pecans. Make the sauce in advance and leave it covered at room temperature.

1½ cups	sugar
1¼ cups	heavy cream
½ teaspoon	pure vanilla extract
2 pints	vanilla ice cream
2 pints	butter pecan ice cream
	toasted pecans (see page 78)

If the sauce gets too thick, reheat it in the microwave.

For the caramel, mix ⅓ cup water and the sugar in a medium heavy-bottomed saucepan. Cook, without stirring, over low heat for 5 to 10 minutes, until the sugar dissolves. Increase the heat to medium and boil uncovered until the sugar turns a warm chestnut brown (about 350 degrees on a candy thermometer), 5 to 7 minutes, gently swirling the pan to stir the mixture. Be careful; the mixture is extremely hot! Watch the mixture constantly at the end, as it will go from caramel to burnt very quickly. Turn off the heat. Stand back to avoid splattering and slowly add the cream and vanilla. The cream will bubble violently and the caramel will solidify; don't worry. Simmer over low heat, stirring constantly, until the caramel dissolves and the sauce is smooth, about 2 minutes. Allow to cool to room temperature, at least 4 hours. It will thicken as it sits.

To assemble the sundaes, place one scoop of vanilla ice cream and one scoop of butter pecan ice cream in each dish and sprinkle with toasted pecans. Drizzle with caramel sauce and serve extra sauce on the side.

breakfast

tri-berry muffins

cranberry orange scones

chunky banana bran muffins

easy cheese danish

omelet for two

scrambled eggs & salmon

maple-roasted bacon

breakfast fruit crunch

sunday morning oatmeal

blueberry crumb cake

anna's orange marmalade

irish soda bread

fresh peach bellinis

spicy bloody marys

designing a kitchen

As a caterer, I worked in lots of home kitchens and believe me, I've seen them all. Some of the worst, I'm afraid to say, are designed by architects who value style over function. First things first: a kitchen has to work. The refrigerator might look great flush with the cabinets, but then there's no place to put down the milk while you hunt for the orange juice behind it. I always design the function first and then work on the style.

The most important element of kitchen design is the work triangle. You want the stove, the sink, and the refrigerator placed in a triangle with enough counter space in between to work, but not so much that you need roller skates to get around. If you have room for an island, put the sink or the stove in the island with the other two appliances opposite and the triangle will work really well. I also think it's really important for the work space to be out of the normal flow of traffic in the house. My kitchen has two doors: the door to the dining room and the door to the garden. My work space is defined by an island parallel to a long wall of cabinets, countertop, and stove. If someone wants to go from the house to the garden, he or she doesn't have to walk through my work space to get there; the passageway is on the other side of the island. There are also lots of places for friends to hang out—the kitchen table and stools so

they can be with me in the kitchen but at the same time outside of my work space.

Contrary to the belief that a large kitchen is always better than a small one, I actually think a medium-size space works best. The work space can be in a larger room but all of the cabinets and equipment should be in one area. My counters are about ten feet long and the aisle is only four feet wide; if the aisle were wider, I'd have to walk farther to put the groceries away or make a cup of tea.

Last, I always think about the view. I spend most of my time in the kitchen washing and chopping, so I positioned the sink and the butcher block with a dead-on view of the kitchen garden behind the house. If you spend most of your time in the kitchen in the morning, try to have it face east . . . or if you are cooking in the afternoons you'll want it to face west. I work there all day long, so mine faces south for the longest exposure to sunlight.

Of course, we all have a dream kitchen in our minds and we all have to compromise. All my life I'd wanted a separate pantry and now, after building so many kitchens, I finally have one. For my next kitchen, I'd love a screened dining porch and a wood-burning oven. But my guide for kitchens is the same as for cooking: keep it simple and make sure you're planning a space in which to have a very good time.

tri-berry muffins

MAKES 16 TO 18 MUFFINS

A cookbook that I turn to often is Sarah Leah Chase's Open House Cookbook. *She made these muffins for me one day and explained that the cook at her specialty food store on Nantucket——after a late night!— accidentally forgot to add the sugar to the batter. She threw it in at the last minute and realized that the muffins came out with a delicious crunchy outside. I love when accidents turn out better than the original.*

3 cups	all-purpose flour
1 tablespoon	baking powder
½ teaspoon	baking soda
½ teaspoon	kosher salt
1½ tablespoons	ground cinnamon
1¼ cups	milk
2	extra-large eggs, lightly beaten
½ pound (2 sticks)	unsalted butter, melted
1 cup	fresh blueberries
½ cup	fresh raspberries
½ cup	diced fresh strawberries
1½ cups	sugar

Preheat the oven to 375 degrees. Line muffin tins with paper liners.

Sift the flour, baking powder, baking soda, salt, and cinnamon together in a large bowl. Stir with your hand to be sure the ingredients are combined. In another bowl, combine the milk, eggs, and melted butter. Make a well in the middle of the dry mixture, pour the wet mixture into the well, and stir until just combined. There will be some lumps but don't overmix the batter! Add the blueberries, raspberries, strawberries, and sugar and stir gently to combine.

Using a 2¼-inch ice cream scoop, spoon the batter into the muffin cups to fill the liners. Bake for 20 to 25 minutes, until a cake tester comes out clean and the tops are nicely browned.

cranberry orange scones

MAKES 14 TO 16 SCONES

At Barefoot Contessa we made all kinds of scones—and they were all delicious. It's the pieces of butter in the dough that make the difference between light and flaky scones and those hockey pucks we've all had at one time or another. You want to be sure that the butter isn't completely incorporated into the dough but rather cut up in small pieces through-out. When the heat of the oven hits the butter, the water in the butter evaporates, creating steam and making the scones light and flaky.

I use Ocean Spray or American Spoon Fruit dried cranberries.

Don't be tempted to use fresh cranberries; they're too tart.

4 cups plus ¼ cup	all-purpose flour
¼ cup	granulated sugar, plus extra for sprinkling
2 tablespoons	baking powder
2 teaspoons	kosher salt
2 teaspoons	grated orange zest (2 oranges)
¾ pound (3 sticks)	cold unsalted butter, diced
4	extra-large eggs, lightly beaten
1 cup (½ pint)	cold heavy cream
1 cup	dried cranberries
1	egg beaten with 2 tablespoons water, for egg wash
½ cup plus 2 tablespoons	confectioners' sugar
4 teaspoons	freshly squeezed orange juice

Preheat the oven to 400 degrees. Line a sheet pan with parchment paper.

In the bowl of an electric mixer fitted with a paddle attachment, mix 4 cups of flour, ¼ cup of granulated sugar, the baking powder, salt, and orange zest. Add the cold butter and mix at the lowest speed until the butter is the size of peas. Combine the eggs and heavy cream and, with the mixer on low speed, slowly add to the flour and butter mixture. Mix until just blended.

The dough will look lumpy! Combine the dried cranberries and ¼ cup of flour, add to the dough, and mix on low speed until blended.

Dump the dough onto a well-floured board and knead it into a ball. Flour your hands and a rolling pin and roll the dough just under 1-inch thick. You should see small bits of butter in the dough. Keep moving the dough on the floured board so it doesn't stick. Flour a 3-inch round plain or fluted cutter and cut circles of dough. Place the scones on the prepared sheet pan. Collect the scraps neatly, roll them out, and cut more circles.

Brush the tops of the scones with the egg wash, sprinkle with granulated sugar, and bake for 20 to 25 minutes, until the tops are browned and the insides are fully baked. The scones will be firm to the touch. Allow the scones to cool for 15 minutes and then whisk together the confectioners' sugar and orange juice and drizzle over the scones.

chunky banana
bran muffins

MAKES 20 TO 24 MUFFINS

Why are most bran muffins so dry and tasteless? I decided to roll up my sleeves and see if I could come up with a bran muffin that's really moist, so I filled it with chunky bananas, raisins, and walnuts. Your family won't even know these muffins are good for them!

2 cups	unprocessed wheat bran
2 cups	buttermilk, shaken
¼ pound (1 stick)	unsalted butter, at room temperature
½ cup	light brown sugar, lightly packed
4	extra-large eggs, at room temperature
¾ cup	unsulfured molasses
2 teaspoons	grated orange zest
1 teaspoon	pure vanilla extract
3 cups	all-purpose flour
1½ teaspoons	baking powder
½ teaspoon	baking soda
1 teaspoon	kosher salt
2 cups	raisins
2 cups	large-diced banana (2 bananas)
1 cup	chopped walnuts

Preheat the oven to 350 degrees. Line muffin tins with paper liners.

Combine the bran and buttermilk and set aside. Cream the butter and sugar in the bowl of an electric mixer fitted with a paddle attachment on a high speed for about 5 minutes, until light and fluffy. With the mixer on low, add the eggs, one at a time. Scrape the bowl and then add the molasses, orange zest, and vanilla. (The mixture will look curdled.) Add the bran-buttermilk mixture and combine.

In a separate bowl, sift together the flour, baking powder, baking soda, and salt. With the mixer on low speed, slowly add the flour mixture to the batter and mix just until combined. Don't overmix it! Fold in the raisins, bananas, and walnuts with a rubber spatula.

With an ice cream scoop or large spoon, fill the muffin cups full and bake for 25 to 30 minutes, until a cake tester comes out clean. Cool in pans.

easy cheese danish

MAKES 8 DANISH

We made these Danish for years at Barefoot Contessa and I thought I'd lost the recipe. I came across it recently among some old papers and I was so happy to have it again. You can assemble these the night before and bake them before breakfast.

8 ounces	cream cheese, at room temperature
⅓ cup	sugar
2	extra-large egg yolks, at room temperature
2 tablespoons	ricotta cheese
1 teaspoon	pure vanilla extract
¼ teaspoon	kosher salt
1 tablespoon	grated lemon zest (2 lemons)
2 sheets (1 box)	frozen puff pastry, defrosted
1	egg beaten with 1 tablespoon of water, for egg wash

Preheat the oven to 400 degrees. Line a sheet pan with parchment paper.

Place the cream cheese and sugar in the bowl of an electric mixer fitted with a paddle attachment and cream them together on low speed until smooth. With the mixer still on low, add the egg yolks, ricotta, vanilla, salt, and lemon zest and mix until just combined. Don't whip!

Unfold one sheet of puff pastry onto a lightly floured board and roll it slightly with a floured rolling pin until it's a 10 × 10-inch square. Cut the sheet into quarters with a sharp knife. Place a heaping tablespoon of cheese filling into the middle of each of the 4 squares. Brush the border of each pastry with egg wash and fold two opposite corners to the center, brushing and overlapping the corners of each pastry so they firmly stick together. Brush the top of the pastries with egg wash. Place the pastries on the prepared sheet pan. Repeat with the second sheet of puff pastry and refrigerate the filled Danish for 15 minutes.

Bake the pastries for about 20 minutes, rotating the pan once during baking, until puffed and brown. Serve warm.

If you make these in advance, reheat them in a 350-degree oven for 5 minutes.

omelet for two

Individual omelets for breakfast are annoying because you have to cook them one at a time. A big frittata solves that problem, but it's a lot of cutting and chopping for two people. So, I decided to try making one big omelet in the oven and came up with a delicious Sunday breakfast that Jeffrey and I can enjoy at the same time. Niman Ranch bacon and good sharp Vermont Cheddar make it even better, if you can find them.

¼ pound	good thick-cut bacon
1 tablespoon	unsalted butter
1 cup	medium-diced Yukon Gold potato
½ cup	chopped yellow onion
1 tablespoon	minced jalapeño pepper
5	extra-large eggs
2 tablespoons	milk or cream
1 teaspoon	kosher salt
½ teaspoon	freshly ground black pepper
¼ cup	chopped scallions, white and green parts
4 ounces	extra-sharp Cheddar, diced, plus grated cheese for garnish

Don't pour bacon grease down the sink; it will clog the drain when it cools. Pour it into an old metal can and discard with the trash.

The heat of a jalapeño is in the seeds and the white membranes. Remove them carefully and be sure to wash your hands.

Preheat the oven to 350 degrees.

Cut the bacon crosswise in 1-inch pieces. Cook the bacon in an 8-inch ovenproof sauté pan over medium-low heat for 5 to 7 minutes, stirring occasionally, until browned. Drain the bacon on paper towels and discard the fat from the pan. Add the butter to the pan, then add the potato and yellow onion. Cook over medium-low heat for about 10 minutes, tossing occasionally, until the onion starts to brown and the potato is tender but firm. Add the jalapeño pepper and cook for 30 seconds.

Meanwhile, in a medium bowl beat the eggs, milk, salt, and pepper together with a fork. Stir in the scallions and diced Cheddar. When the potato is cooked, add the bacon to the pan and pour over the egg mixture. Place the pan in the oven for 15 to 20 minutes, until the omelet puffs and the eggs are almost cooked in the center. Sprinkle with a handful of grated Cheddar and bake for another minute. Serve hot directly from the pan.

scrambled eggs & salmon

SERVES 4 TO 5

I love the idea of smoked salmon with eggs (the old-fashioned Jewish dish is called L.E.O.—lox, eggs, and onions), but there's something about the taste and texture of cooked smoked salmon that I don't love. So I decided to add the salmon after the eggs were cooked and now it's one of our favorite Sunday morning breakfasts.

4 tablespoons (½ stick)	unsalted butter, divided
½ cup	chopped shallots (3 to 4 shallots)
12	extra-large eggs
6 tablespoons	half-and-half
1 teaspoon	kosher salt
½ teaspoon	freshly ground black pepper
2 tablespoons	chopped fresh chives
1 tablespoon	chopped fresh flat-leaf parsley
4 ounces	sliced smoked salmon, julienned

I prefer Norwegian or Scottish smoked salmon because they tend to be less oily and less salty. To julienne, stack the slices, roll them like a cigarette, and slice crosswise ½ inch thick.

Melt 2 tablespoons butter in a large (12-inch) sauté pan over medium-low heat. Add the shallots and cook for 5 to 7 minutes, tossing frequently, until the shallots are translucent and they begin to brown.

Meanwhile, in a large bowl, beat together the eggs, half-and-half, salt, and pepper with a fork. When the shallots are cooked, add the eggs to the pan and cook over medium-low heat for 4 to 5 minutes, stirring frequently with a rubber spatula to scrape the bottom and sides of the pan, lifting and folding the eggs to make large curds. Remove from the heat 1 minute before they're completely done because they'll continue cooking in the pan. Off the heat, add the remaining 2 tablespoons of butter, chives, parsley, and smoked salmon. Mix well, season to taste, and serve hot.

maple-roasted bacon

SERVES 4 TO 8

Everyone knows how to cook bacon but I have two special tricks: first, the bacon roasts in the oven on a rack so you don't have to keep turning it in the pan; and second, you brush it with maple syrup at the end to give it great flavor. The best ingredients—thick-cut bacon and Grade A dark amber maple syrup—really do make a difference.

¾ pound	thick-cut smoked bacon (16 slices)
1 to 2 tablespoons	good maple syrup

Preheat the oven to 400 degrees.

Place a baking rack on a sheet pan and arrange the bacon in one layer on the baking rack. Bake for 15 to 20 minutes, until the bacon begins to brown. Remove the pan carefully from the oven—there will be hot grease in the pan! Brush the bacon slices with maple syrup and bake for another 3 to 5 minutes, until the bacon is a warm golden brown. Transfer the bacon to a plate lined with paper towels and serve warm.

breakfast fruit crunch

SERVES 4

I use Quaker or McCann's oatmeal— old-fashioned or quick-cooking.

Golden pineapples are a variety that is sweeter than regular pineapples. You can find them all year round in grocery and specialty produce stores.

Brussels is one of my favorite cities and Pain Quotidien, which started there and now has shops in New York and L.A., is one of my favorite restaurants. One Sunday morning, everyone there was having what looked like ice cream sundaes for breakfast so, of course, I had to order one. It turned out to be a delicious—and healthy!— parfait of fresh fruit, yogurt, and granola.

1 cup	old-fashioned or quick-cooking (not instant) oatmeal
½ cup	sweetened, shredded coconut
½ cup	sliced or slivered almonds
3 tablespoons	vegetable oil
2 tablespoons	honey
8 to 10	strawberries, diced
½ cup	blueberries
¼	fresh pineapple, preferably golden, diced
2 cups	plain yogurt

Preheat the oven to 350 degrees.

To make the granola, toss the oatmeal, coconut, almonds, oil, and honey together in a large bowl until they are completely combined. Pour onto a sheet pan and bake, stirring occasionally with a metal spatula, until the mixture turns an even golden brown, about 20 minutes.

Remove the granola from the oven, scrape the pan with the spatula to loosen the granola, and allow to cool, stirring once.

Combine the strawberries, blueberries, and pineapple in a bowl. In 4 parfait glasses or tall glasses, alternately layer half the fruit, then half the yogurt, and sprinkle with the cooled granola. Repeat with a second layer of fruit, yogurt, and granola.

sunday morning oatmeal

SERVES 4

This is my favorite winter breakfast, especially when we have house-guests. I make it with McCann's quick-cooking oatmeal and it's so satisfying.

1½ cups	whole milk, plus extra for serving
1½ cups	quick-cooking (not instant) oatmeal
½ teaspoon	kosher salt
1	banana, sliced
½ cup	dried cherries
½ cup	golden raisins
	pure maple syrup or brown sugar, for serving

Don't cut the banana in advance or it will turn brown.

Heat the milk plus 2 cups water in a medium saucepan until it starts to simmer. Add the oatmeal and salt, bring to a boil, then lower the heat and simmer for 4 to 5 minutes, stirring occasionally, until thickened. Off the heat, stir in the banana, cherries, and raisins. Place the lid on the pot and allow to sit for 2 minutes. Serve hot with maple syrup or brown sugar and extra milk.

blueberry crumb cake

SERVES 6 TO 8

I used to love the old-fashioned crumb cakes that my grandmother bought in Brooklyn bakeries. This cake is as close as I could come to my memory of that flavor and texture.

For the streusel

¼ cup	granulated sugar
⅓ cup	light brown sugar, lightly packed
1 teaspoon	ground cinnamon
⅛ teaspoon	ground nutmeg
¼ pound (1 stick)	unsalted butter, melted
1⅓ cups	all-purpose flour

For the cake

6 tablespoons (¾ stick)	unsalted butter, at room temperature
¾ cups	granulated sugar
2	extra-large eggs, at room temperature
1 teaspoon	pure vanilla extract
½ teaspoon	grated lemon zest
⅔ cup	sour cream
1¼ cups	all-purpose flour
1 teaspoon	baking powder
¼ teaspoon	baking soda
½ teaspoon	kosher salt
1 cup	fresh blueberries
	confectioners' sugar, for sprinkling

Preheat the oven to 350 degrees. Butter and flour a 9-inch round baking pan.

For the streusel, combine the granulated sugar, brown sugar, cinnamon, and nutmeg in a bowl. Stir in the melted butter and then the flour. Mix well and set aside.

For the cake, cream the butter and sugar in the bowl of an electric mixer fitted with the paddle attachment on high speed for 4 to 5 minutes, until light. Reduce the speed to low and add the eggs one at a time, then add the vanilla, lemon zest, and sour cream. In a separate bowl, sift together the flour, baking powder, baking soda, and salt. With the mixer on low speed, add the flour mixture to the batter until just combined. Fold in the blueberries and stir with a spatula to be sure the batter is completely mixed.

Spoon the batter into the prepared pan and spread it out with a knife. With your fingers, crumble the topping evenly over the batter. Bake for 40 to 50 minutes, until a cake tester comes out clean. Cool completely and serve sprinkled with confectioners' sugar.

anna's orange marmalade

MAKES 3 TO 4 PINTS

This is my absolute favorite orange marmalade. It's the recipe from Anna Pump's Country Weekend Entertaining *cookbook and it's so popular at her store, Loaves & Fishes, that you have to order it in advance to be sure you can get some. It's not too sweet and not too tart; it's easy to make and you'll have enough to give away as hostess gifts.*

4 large	seedless oranges
2	lemons
8 cups	sugar

Sterilize the jars and sealing lids by running them through a cycle—without soap—in the dishwasher.

A simmer is a very low boil; you will see bubbles just breaking the surface.

The marmalade will be a little runny the first day, but it will set as it sits in the jar.

Cut the oranges and lemons in half crosswise, then into very thin half-moon slices. (If you have a mandoline, this will be quite fast.) Discard any seeds. Place the sliced fruit and their juices into a stainless-steel pot. Add 8 cups water and bring the mixture to a boil, stirring often. Remove from the heat and stir in the sugar until it dissolves. Cover and allow to stand overnight at room temperature.

The next day, bring the mixture back to a boil. Reduce the heat to low and simmer uncovered for 2 hours. Turn the heat up to medium and boil gently, stirring often, for another 30 minutes. Skim off any foam that forms on the top. Cook the marmalade until it reaches 220 degrees. If you want to be doubly sure it's ready, place a small amount on a plate and refrigerate it until it's cool but not cold. If it's firm—neither runny nor hard—it's done. It will be a golden orange color. (If the marmalade is runny, continue cooking it and if it's hard, add more water.)

Pour the marmalade into clean, hot Mason jars; wipe the rims thoroughly with a clean damp paper towel; and seal with the lids. Store in the pantry for up to a year.

irish soda bread

MAKES 1 LOAF

Irish soda bread is a really easy way to have a gorgeous hot bread come out of the oven without dealing with yeast and all those risings. Most soda breads taste pretty bland to me, so I decided to play around and see if I could just turn up the volume on the flavor. Orange zest and currants really did the trick.

4 cups	all-purpose flour, plus extra for the currants
4 tablespoons	sugar (see note)
1 teaspoon	baking soda
1½ teaspoons	kosher salt
4 tablespoons (½ stick)	cold unsalted butter, cut into ½-inch dice
1¾ cups	cold buttermilk, shaken
1	extra-large egg, lightly beaten
1 teaspoon	grated orange zest
1 cup	dried currants

If you like Irish soda bread less sweet, reduce the sugar to 2 or 3 tablespoons.

Preheat the oven to 375 degrees. Line a sheet pan with parchment paper.

Combine the flour, sugar, baking soda, and salt in the bowl of an electric mixer fitted with a paddle attachment. Add the butter and mix on low speed until the butter is mixed into the flour.

With a fork, lightly beat the buttermilk, egg, and orange zest together in a measuring cup. With the mixer on low speed, slowly add the buttermilk mixture to the flour mixture. Combine the currants with 1 tablespoon of flour and mix into the dough. It will be very wet.

Dump the dough onto a well-floured board and knead it a few times into a round loaf. Place the loaf on the prepared sheet pan and lightly cut an X into the top of the bread with a serrated knife. Bake for 45 to 55 minutes, or until a cake tester comes out clean. When you tap the loaf, it will have a hollow sound.

Cool on a baking rack. Serve warm or at room temperature.

fresh peach bellinis

MAKES 6 DRINKS

Harry's Bar in Venice is one of the most famous restaurants in the world. Jeffrey and I were lucky enough to meet the owner, Arrigo Cipriani, and he kindly took us to see his amazing pasta factory on the island of Giudecca. At Harry's Bar the Bellini, a drink named after the Venetian painter Giovanni Bellini, is always made with fresh peach purée.

2	ripe peaches, unpeeled, pitted, and diced
1 tablespoon	freshly squeezed lemon juice
1 teaspoon	sugar
1 bottle (750 ml)	chilled Prosecco sparkling wine

For really quick Bellinis, or when peaches are out of season, you can substitute a good-quality peach nectar, such as Looza or Kerns, for the peach purée.

Place the peaches, lemon juice, and sugar in the bowl of a food processor fitted with a steel blade and process until smooth. Press the mixture through a sieve and discard the peach solids in the sieve. Place 2 tablespoons of the peach purée in each of 6 champagne glasses and fill with cold Prosecco. Serve immediately.

spicy bloody marys

MAKES 6 DRINKS

Most Bloody Marys are just flavored tomato juice and vodka; I like mine with lots of flavor and texture. Puréed fresh celery and lemon juice give this classic drink extra bite.

3 large	celery stalks, plus additional stalks for serving
3 teaspoons	prepared horseradish
2 teaspoons	grated yellow onion
½ cup	freshly squeezed lemon juice (3 lemons)
1 teaspoon	Worcestershire sauce
1 teaspoon	celery salt
½ teaspoon	kosher salt
½ teaspoon	Tabasco, or to taste
1 (46-ounce) can	Sacramento tomato juice
2 cups	vodka

Cut the celery in large dice, including the leaves, and purée in the bowl of a food processor fitted with a steel blade. Add the horseradish, onion, lemon juice, Worcestershire sauce, celery salt, kosher salt, and Tabasco and purée it again. Pour the tomato juice into a 2½-quart container, stir in the celery and seasonings mixture, then add the vodka and chill. Place a few ice cubes in each glass, pour in the Bloody Mary mixture, and garnish with a celery stick.

if you're visiting the hamptons...

There are so many wonderful places to visit in the Hamptons that I can't possibly list all of them, but these are some of my favorites. "The Hamptons" is actually a string of historic villages, including East Hampton, Bridgehampton, and Southampton, on the south coast of Long Island, and each town has its own special character. I hope you'll enjoy visiting these places as much as I do.

specialty foods

Loaves & Fishes

50 Sagg Main Street
Sagaponack

Anna Pump runs one of the best specialty food stores in America, offering take-out dinners, salads, and amazing baked goods. Anna's famous for so many things, but her fresh lobster salad is especially renowned.

Mary's Marvelous

207 Main Street
Amagansett

Mary Schoenlein started with fabulous granola and then expanded into delicious take-out sandwiches and dinners. We love to stop by and get a sandwich and one of her fabulous cookies before heading to the beach.

Cavaniola's Gourmet Cheese Shop

89B Division Street
Sag Harbor

Michael and Tracey Cavaniola opened this amazing cheese shop in 2001 and we're all incredibly grateful. They really understand cheeses and just to smell the air reminds you of the finest cheese shops of France. They're very generous with tastes, so you can learn about cheeses you've never even dreamed of. I love their Neal's Yard Dairy cheeses.

The Seafood Shop

356 Montauk Highway
Wainscott

This wonderful store was started in 1972 by John Haessler and Robert Wilford, and the tradition of local fresh fish and seafood has been continued since 2000 by Colin Mather. They also make clambakes on the beach and wonderful lunches and dinners to take out. I love their lobster rolls.

Claws on Wheels

19 Race Lane
East Hampton

Tony Minardi, a marine biologist, owns this wonderful seafood shop and he recently moved into a larger space. He carries fresh local fish and seafood and also does wonderful clambakes on the beach. I often have their grilled fish or delicious soups for lunch.

Tate's Bake Shop
43 North Sea Road
Southampton

Kathleen King started baking chocolate chip cookies when she was eleven years old and now she's built it into a national baking empire. Tate's Bake Shop is ground zero; everything from the apple pies to the chocolate cakes to the millions of cookies she sells are baked there, and they're absolutely delicious.

farmstands
Iacono Chickens
106 Long Lane
East Hampton

Sal and Eileen Iacono inherited a farm from their family and decided to raise chickens instead of vegetables. And how grateful we all are that they did! Try one Iacono chicken and you'll never get one from the grocery store again. They also sell fresh eggs and, in season, delicious capons and geese.

The Milk Pail Country Store and Mecox Farm
Montauk Highway and Mecox Road
Water Mill

The Halsey family has owned apple and pear orchards for generations. Recently, their daughter Jenn Halsey Dupree started growing delicious peaches, too. I love to go to the farm on Mecox Road and pick my own apples, but if I'm in a hurry, the store on Montauk Highway is open from September to April. They specialize in many varieties of heirloom apples and they're all delicious.

Mecox Bay Dairy
855 Mecox Road
Bridgehampton

I first tasted cheeses from Mecox Bay Dairy at a small farmer's market that started recently in Sag Harbor. Arthur Ludlow makes wonderful cheeses at his farm in Water Mill.

The Green Thumb
Montauk Highway
Water Mill

I've been shopping at the Halseys' wonderful farm store since 1978 and it's as good as ever. They grow all kinds of salad greens, vegetables, and herbs; their heirloom tomatoes and beans are really amazing. Even in summer traffic, it's always worth the trip from East Hampton.

Jim and Jennifer Pike
Sagg Main Street
Sagaponack
Jim Pike grew up in New York's
Westchester County and dreamed
of being a farmer, so he moved to
Bridgehampton and started growing the most wonderful vegetables. Visiting Jennifer at their
stand is truly one of my great
pleasures. They're best known for
their corn, tomatoes, and basil,
but their vegetables and melons
are truly special, too.

Round Swamp Farm
184 Three Mile Harbor Road
East Hampton
Carolyn Snyder started this wonderful farm store with a full range
of produce and local fish. Now she
and her daughter Lisa have
expanded into prepared soups,
dinners, and baked goods to take
out. This really is a local staple
because in one stop you can find
everything for dinner: fish and
seafood, salads and vegetables,
and delectable homemade cakes
and cookies for dessert.

cookware and tableware
Loaves & Fishes Cookshop
2422 Montauk Highway
Bridgehampton
Sybille Pump Van Kempen used to
run the specialty food store
Loaves & Fishes with her mother,
Anna. She and her husband, Ger-
rit Van Kempen, decided to open
this amazing cookware store on
Main Street in Bridgehampton.
They sell every kind of high-
quality cookware imaginable, plus
wonderful tableware and platters.

Mecox Gardens
257 County Road 39A
Southampton

66 Newtown Lane
East Hampton
When Mac Hoak decided he'd
had enough of investment bank-
ing, he moved to Southampton to
open a wonderful interior and garden store. It's a great place to find
beautiful outdoor furniture and
that perfect dining table you've
always wanted. They also carry
wonderful accessories and books
for the home.

H. Groome
9 Main Street
Southampton
Whenever I need something
great-looking for my house or the
table, I head for H. Groome.
Everything there is gorgeous and
very chic. I'm particularly crazy
about the table linens and their
wonderful selection of glass vases
and votive candle holders from
Belgium.

Bloom
**43 Madison Street at Sage
Street**
Sag Harbor
Mona Nerenberg simply has great
taste. I want everything in her
store, from antique tables to
chairs, to framed photographs and
outdoor furniture. Mona also sells
wonderful handmade tableware
and platters that you'll need to
buy. All the designers flock here.

Monogram Shop
7 Newtown Lane
East Hampton
Valerie Smith has an amazing eye
for really beautiful things. She
started this store selling antiques
and all kinds of terrific things like
canvas bags and towels to monogram on the spot plus personalized stationery and note pads.
Over the years, she's added the
best children's clothes you can
imagine and lots of tableware that
I can't resist. This is the best
place to find that perfect gift.

Turpan
55 Main Street
East Hampton
In the 1980s, Greg Turpan founded one of the most famous houseware stores in New York, called Turpan-Sanders. Now, fortunately for me, he's moved to East Hampton and runs this wonderful store with his wife, Katherine. They choose the best of everything for the house and it's all modern and very cool. I love their champagne glasses.

Sage Street Antiques
Sage Street
Sag Harbor
Liza Warner is an institution in the Hamptons. Every Saturday morning a line forms outside her door, waiting for her to open. This store is chock full of wonderful country antiques, collectibles, and even antique cookware and linens. You can't walk away empty-handed.

Sylvester & Company
Main Street
Sag Harbor
Linda Sylvester has assembled a charming and personal collection of tableware and a few pantry products plus coffee and cookies to snack on while you browse. You can find anything from a personalized dog bowl for the family pet, to utensils and cookware for Asian cooking, to beautiful serving platters. This is a great place to find the unusual gift you wouldn't see anywhere else.

florists
Bridgehampton Florist
2400 Montauk Highway
Bridgehampton
Michael Grimm and Jim Osborne started this wonderful flower shop years ago, and it's as good as ever. You can buy armloads of local flowers in the summer and beautiful imported flowers all year long. They also make gorgeous arrangements to send to that special someone.

Amagansett Flowers by Beth
154 Main Street
Amagansett
Beth Eckhardt does beautiful flower arrangements for both small parties and large events. Her tiny shop is crowded not only with beautiful flowers to buy by the stem but also with wonderful tableware to spice up any party.

favorite places to visit
Main Beach, East Hampton
There's a beautiful pavillion at this beach at the end of Main Street (called Ocean Avenue) that's a wonderful place to sit and watch the waves crash. In summer, the snack bar also makes hot dogs and lobster rolls to eat on a blanket on the sand.

Town Pond, East Hampton

A long time ago when there were no cars or roads in eastern Long Island, the farmers used to walk their cattle from East Hampton to Montauk (quite a long trip!), to graze. The town pond was no doubt a place for the cattle to get a drink along the way. Now, it's populated by ducks and swans that look as though they were sent in by central casting. We love to take bread down to the pond to feed them.

Mulford Farm

10 James Lane
East Hampton

This circa 1680 farm in the heart of East Hampton Village is considered one of America's most significant—and intact—colonial farmsteads. Largely unchanged since 1750, the restored house, barn, and garden are an amazing reminder of colonial life. Next door is the Home Sweet Home museum, about which the song was wrtten.

Duryea's Lobster Deck

65 Tuthill Road
Montauk

This is the best-kept secret in the Hamptons. For lunch or dinner, Duryea's is the real thing, with paper plates and big umbrellas, and the food is absolutely delicious. I love to sit with an order of grilled fish or lobster salad and watch the sailboats go out to sea. If you come early for dinner, you'll also get a beautiful view of the sun setting over the Long Island Sound.

Candy Kitchen

Main Street
Bridgehampton

This is the classic old-fashioned luncheonette with delicious food where investment bankers and farmers all sit at the counter together to enjoy the grilled cheese sandwiches and home-made ice cream. Gus Laggis, the owner, also makes wonderful Greek specialties like souvlaki and Greek salads with pita bread.

credits

Unless otherwise specified, tableware and linens shown in the photographs are privately owned.

page 24
yellow bowl from
Global Table
107–109 Sullivan Street
New York, NY 10012
212-431-5839

pages 50 and 222
white plates from
Bloom
43 Madison Street
Sag Harbor, NY 11963
631-725-5940

page 65
heirloom tomatoes from
Melissas.com or
800-588-0151

pages 76 and 139
white bowl and
wood tray from
Crate and Barrel
800-967-6696

pages 145, 148, and 151
gratin dishes and
Dutch oven from
Le Creuset
877-273-8738

page 169
orange napkins from
H. Groome
9 Main Street
Southampton, NY 11968
631-204-0491

page 179
plates from
Ted Muehling
27 Howard Street
New York, NY 10013
212-431-3825

menus

summer breakfast
omelet for two
cranberry orange scones
blueberries & honeydew melon
iced coffee

birthday breakfast
scrambled eggs & salmon
toasted honey white bread
anna's orange marmalade
fresh peach bellinis

holiday breakfast
scrambled eggs
maple-roasted bacon
tri-berry muffins
spicy bloody marys

lunch in the garden
chicken salad sandwiches
heirloom tomatoes with
  blue cheese dressing
lemon yogurt cake
fresh blueberries

autumn lunch
fresh pea soup
chicken salad véronique
pita bread
sliced tomatoes and basil
panna cotta with balsamic strawberries

mediterranean feast
lamb kebabs
couscous with pine nuts
tomato feta salad
pita bread
store-bought hummus
summer fruit crostata

working lunch
fresh pea soup
caesar club sandwich
tomato feta salad
ultimate ginger cookie

holiday dinner
green herb dip with crudités
capon with roast carrots
buttermilk mashed potatoes
pumpkin mousse parfait

winter dinner by the fire
loin of pork with fennel
orange-honey glazed carrots
creamy rosemary polenta
caramel pecan sundaes

dinner in the garden
fresh whiskey sours
chicken with goat cheese & basil
summer garden pasta
chocolate sorbet

summer bbq
salsa & chips
blue cheese burgers
guacamole salad
peach & blueberry crumbles

boss comes to dinner
fresh whiskey sours
bibb salad with basil green goddess dressing
seafood gratin
mixed berry pavlova
demi-sec champagne

For menus using recipes from all five Barefoot Contessa cookbooks.
please go to barefootcontessa.com.

index

recipe index